1,001 FACTS ABOUT QUARTERBACKS

Luke Glancy

Jim Plunkett

Jim Kelly

1,001 FACTS ABOUT QUARTERBACKS

Michael Vick

BY MATT MARINI

DK Publishing, Inc.

LONDON, NEW YORK, MELBOURNE,
MUNICH, AND DELHI

Project Editor Elizabeth Hester
Senior Art Editor Michelle Baxter
Publisher Chuck Lang
Creative Director Tina Vaughan
Production Chris Avgherinos

NFL CREATIVE
Editor-in-Chief John Wiebusch
Managing Editor John Fawaz
Project Art Director Bill Madrid
Director–Manufacturing Dick Falk
Director–Print Services Tina Dahl
Manager–Computer Graphics Sandy Gordon

First American Edition, 2003
2 4 6 8 10 9 7 5 3 1

Published in the United States by DK Publishing, Inc.
375 Hudson Street, New York, New York 10014

A catalog record for this book is available from the Library of Congress.

ISBN: 0-7894-9860-X

DK Publishing books are available at special discounts for bulk purchases for sales promotions or premiums.
Special editions, including personalized covers, excerpts of existing guides, and corporate imprints can be
created in large quantities for specific needs. For more information, contact Special Markets Dept./
DK Publishing, Inc./375 Hudson Street/New York, New York 10014/FAX: 800-600-9098.

Color reproduction by Hong Kong Scanner
Printed in Singapore by Star Standard

Discover more at
www.dk.com

CONTENTS

SUPER BOWL
STARS

TROY AIKMAN

Ht: 6'4" Wt: 219 Pro Career: 1989–2000

Playing quarterback for the Dallas Cowboys is a pressure job— and going 0–11 as a rookie starter only makes things worse. Troy Aikman, the first player picked in the 1989 draft, became the first rookie quarterback to start a season opener for the club since 1969. But Dallas knew it had a winner, and it was correct. Aikman's 90 regular-season victories during the 1990s are the most by a quarterback in one decade. He led the Cowboys to three Super Bowl titles (XXVII, XXVIII, and XXX) while completing a Super Bowl-record 70 percent of his passes. He is the Cowboys' career leader in passing yards and touchdowns.

Born: 11/21/66
Hometown: West Covina, CA
College: UCLA
NFL Draft: 1st Round, 1989

Aikman Trivia: In what 1996 movie did Troy make a cameo appearance as himself?

TERRY BRADSHAW

Ht: 6'3" Wt: 215 Pro Career: 1970-1983

Today, fans know Terry Bradshaw as a popular pregame studio host. He's come a long way since the early 1970s, when Steelers fans showered boos (among other items) on the first-round draft pick. The boos continued in 1972, even though he guided the Steelers to the first postseason victory in the franchise's 40-year history. Finally, in 1974, Bradshaw became the permanent starter, and he proceeded to lead the Steelers to an unprecedented four Super Bowl titles (IX, X, XIII, and XIV) during the next six seasons. Known for his deep-passing ability and go-for-broke mentality, Bradshaw averaged a record 11.1 yards per attempt in the Super Bowl, including touchdown bombs of 64, 75, 47, and 73 yards.

Born: 9/2/48
Hometown: Shreveport, LA
College: Louisiana Tech
NFL Draft: 1st Round, 1970

Bradshaw Trivia: *Terry was the second player to win consecutive Super Bowl MVP awards (in games XIII and XIV). Who was the first?*

JOHN ELWAY

Ht: 6'3" Wt: 215 Pro Career: 1983–1998

John Elway, a multi-sport star, pitched his high school baseball team to the Los Angeles city championship. But this son of a football coach shined brightest on the gridiron. The first player picked in the 1983 NFL Draft, Elway led the Broncos to five Super Bowls, including victories in games XXXII and XXXIII. He was best known for his strong right arm and his knack for last-second heroics, including "The Drive," a 98-yard fourth-quarter march in the 1986 AFC Championship Game against Cleveland. Elway directed 33 fourth-quarter comeback victories during his career.

Born: 6/28/60
Hometown: Port Angeles, WA
College: Stanford
NFL Draft: 1st Round, 1983

Elway Trivia: *For which major-league organization did John play one season of minor league baseball in Oneonta, New York in 1982?*

BOB GRIESE

Ht: 6'1" Wt: 190 Pro Career: 1967–1980

Bob Griese does not rank in the top 10 of any of the NFL's career passing charts, but he nearly always played on winning teams. He was a two-time All-America pick at Purdue, where he led the club to a Rose Bowl crown. He was the Dolphins' first-round pick in 1967, in just the club's second year of existence, and he guided the franchise to its most successful decade. Griese led Miami to three consecutive Super Bowls, posting back-to-back victories in games VII and VIII. He was selected to eight Pro Bowls and inducted into the Pro Football Hall of Fame in 1990.

Born: 2/3/45
Hometown: Evansville, IN
College: Purdue
NFL Draft: 1st Round, 1967

iese Trivia: *Bob was one of two _ue_ products to become a starting _rback_ for a Super Bowl champion _ho_ was the other?*

JOE MONTANA

Ht: *6'2"* **Wt:** *200* **Pro Career:** *1979–1994*

Despite a spectacular career at Notre Dame, Joe Montana lasted until the third round of the 1979 draft. That's when new 49ers coach Bill Walsh selected Montana, believing the youngster could run his revolutionary West Coast offense. The short passing game, predicated upon timing and quick decisions, was the perfect fit for his skills. He became the starter in 1981 and guided the 49ers to victory in four Super Bowls. Montana saved his best for the big game—he was never intercepted in the Super Bowl, tossed a record 11 touchdowns, and is the only player to have won the game's MVP award three times.

Born: *6/11/56*
Hometown: *New Eagle, PA*
College: *Notre Dame*
NFL Draft: *3rd Round, 1979*

Montana Trivia: *Name the three quarterbacks selected before Joe in the 1979 NFL Draft.*

JIM PLUNKETT

Ht: 6'3" Wt: 220 Pro Career: 1971–1986

Jim Plunkett, who won the Heisman Trophy as a senior at Stanford, was selected by the New England Patriots with the first overall pick of the 1971 NFL Draft. But success in pro football did not come easily. He was traded to the 49ers in 1976 and released after the 1977 season. The Raiders claimed him, but he did not start until Dan Pastorini suffered an injury during the 1980 season. With Plunkett as the starter, the Raiders finished 9–2 and became the first wild-card team to win a Super Bowl (XV), and Plunkett won MVP honors. He also guided the Raiders to the Super Bowl XVIII title.

Born: 12/5/47
Hometown: San Jose, CA
College: Stanford
NFL Draft: 1st Round, 1971

Plunkett Trivia: *What player caught Jim's Super Bowl record 80-yard touchdown pass in Super Bowl XV?*

BART STARR

Ht: 6'1" Wt: 197 Pro Career: 1956–1971

The Packers didn't know what they had. Green Bay didn't select Bart Starr until the seventeenth round of the 1956 draft, and three seasons later, Starr still split time at quarterback. Only after Vince Lombardi was hired as coach in 1959 did Starr become the full-time starter. From 1960–67, his record as a starter was 82–24–4, and the Packers won five NFL titles and the first two Super Bowls (Starr was named the MVP of both games). Starr coached the Packers for nine seasons (1975–1983), becoming the only starting Super Bowl quarterback later to be an NFL head coach.

Born: 1/9/34
Hometown: Montgomery, AL
College: Alabama
NFL Draft: 17th Round, 1956

Starr Trivia: *Bart is the lowest-drafted quarterback to win a Super Bowl. Which Super Bowl-winning quarterback was not drafted at all?*

DOUG WILLIAMS

Ht: 6'4" Wt: 220 Pro Career: 1978–1989

As the first African-American quarterback drafted in the first round, Doug Williams knocked down barriers. Joining a team that had won two games in two years, Williams led Tampa Bay to the playoffs in 1979 and 1981. He played a few seasons in the USFL before joining the Redskins. In 1987, Williams guided Washington to two playoff victories, and knocked down another barrier by starting Super Bowl XXII. He passed for a record 4 touchdowns in one quarter, and finished with 340 passing yards in the Redskins' 42–10 victory.

Born: 8/9/55
Hometown: Zachary, LA
College: Grambling State
NFL Draft: 1st Round, 1978

Williams Trivia: *Doug was the first African-American to start at quarterback in a Super Bowl. Who was the first African-American quarterback to start a playoff game?*

DOUBLE TROUBLE

AARON BROOKS

Ht: 6'4" Wt: 205 Pro Career: 1999–present

New Orleans acquired Aaron Brooks from Green Bay in 2000, and he quickly made an impact with his arm and his feet. Brooks replaced injured starter Jeff Blake in the twelfth game of the season and immediately orchestrated a 31–24 victory over the Rams, thus becoming just the third quarterback to beat a defending Super Bowl champion in his first start. Brooks later became the first NFL player to have a 400-yard passing game and a 100-yard rushing game in the same season. He also led the Saints to the 2000 playoffs and passed for 4 touchdowns in a 31–28 victory over St. Louis—the franchise's first postseason victory.

Born: 3/24/76
Hometown: Newport News, VA
College: Virginia
NFL Draft: 4th Round, 1999

Brooks Trivia: *Aaron is second cousin to what other star NFL quarterback?*

MARK BRUNELL

Ht: 6'1" Wt: 217 Pro Career: 1993–present

After spending his first two NFL seasons riding Green Bay's bench behind Brett Favre, Mark Brunell went to Jacksonville in a trade, and his career took off. No quarterback has meant more to an expansion franchise than Brunell, who set a record by leading his team in passing in each of its first eight seasons (1995–2002), eclipsing the mark set by Seattle's Jim Zorn. Brunell was chosen to play in the Pro Bowl after the 1996, 1997, and 1999 seasons. In 1996, he passed for 4,367 yards, and in 1999 he led the Jaguars to an NFL-best 14–2 record.

Born: 9/17/70
Hometown: Los Angeles, CA
College: Washington
NFL Draft: 5th Round, 1993

Brunell Trivia: *Mark started 10 of the Jaguars' 16 games in their inaugural 1995 season. Who started the other six games, including the season opener?*

DAUNTE CULPEPPER

Ht: 6'4" Wt: 260 Pro Career: 1999–present

Despite the fact that Daunte Culpepper, the Vikings' 1999 first-round pick, had not thrown a pass in his rookie season, coach Dennis Green made him the starter in 2000. How did Culpepper respond? He rushed for 3 touchdowns in a season-opening win. He was equally productive through the air, posting seven games with 3 touchdown passes, and five 300-yard efforts in 2000 as the Vikings reached the NFC Championship Game. After an injury-plagued 2001 season, Culpepper bounced back in 2002, passing for 3,853 yards and 18 touchdowns, while rushing for 609 yards and 10 scores.

Born: 1/28/77
Hometown: Ocala, FL
College: Central Florida
NFL Draft: 1st Round, 1999

Culpepper Trivia: *Daunte was the eleventh pick of the 1999 draft, but the fourth quarterback chosen. What quarterbacks were drafted earlier?*

RICH GANNON

Ht: *6'3"* **Wt:** *210* **Pro Career:** *1987–present*

Rich Gannon had to wait a while for his NFL career to get on track. Drafted by New England, he was dealt two weeks later to Minnesota, where he was a part-time starter from 1990–92. He was traded to the Washington Redskins in 1993, was out of football in 1994, and played sparingly for three seasons in Kansas City before starting 10 games in 1998. He signed with the Raiders in 1999, and the mobile Gannon has been the perfect field general for Oakland's West Coast offense. He earned NFL MVP honors after his record-setting performance in 2002, when he led Oakland to the AFC title.

Born: *12/20/65*
Hometown: *Philadelphia, PA*
College: *Delaware*
NFL Draft: *4th Round, 1987*

Gannon Trivia: *Rich started 10 games for the Chiefs in 1998. Who started the six other games?*

JEFF GARCIA

Ht: 6'1" Wt: 195 Pro Career: 1994–present

Despite a record-setting collegiate career, Garcia was not drafted by an NFL team in 1994. Jeff played five seasons in the Canadian Football League, earning MVP honors in Calgary's 1998 Grey Cup victory. San Francisco 49ers executive Bill Walsh, who coached against Garcia in college, brought him to San Francisco as Steve Young's backup in 1999. When Young was injured, Jeff became the starter, and the elusive Garcia has been a worthy successor to the 49ers' quarterback legacy. In 2000–01, he became the first player in club history to pass for 30 touchdowns in consecutive seasons.

Born: 2/24/70
Hometown: Gilroy, CA
College: San Jose State
NFL Draft: Free Agent

Garcia Trivia: *Against which team did Jeff engineer a comeback to overcome a 24-point deficit in a 2002 NFC Wild Card Game?*

DONOVAN MCNABB

Ht: **6'2"** *Wt:* **226** *Pro Career:* **1999–present**

With the first pick of the 1999 NFL Draft, the Cleveland Browns selected Tim Couch. With the next pick, the Philadelphia Eagles chose Donovan McNabb. McNabb, who started only six games as a rookie, has been a fixture since, frustrating opponents with his arm and his scrambling. He led the Eagles to three consecutive playoff appearances, even though an injury interrupted his 2002 season (he passed for 4 scores against Arizona in week 11 while playing on what turned out to be a broken ankle). He returned for the playoffs, and guided the Eagles to their second consecutive NFC title game.

Born: **11/25/76**
Hometown: **Chicago, IL**
College: **Syracuse**
NFL Draft: **1st Round, 1999**

McNabb Trivia: *What Pro Bowl defensive end, who also was a top-five first-round pick in the draft, was a high-school teammate of Donovan's?*

STEVE McNAIR

Ht: 6'2" Wt: 225 Pro Career: 1995–present

Not only is Steve McNair one of the toughest players, he is a winner. McNair overcame injuries to help the Titans reach the postseason three times in four seasons (1999–2002). In his first 95 starts, the Titans compiled a 59–36 record (.621 winning percentage). In 1999, McNair missed five weeks after back surgery, but returned to lead the team to Super Bowl XXXIV. In 2002, injuries prevented McNair from practicing much of the season, yet he guided the Titans to the AFC title game. McNair rushed for 64 yards in Super Bowl XXXIV—the most ever by a quarterback in a Super Bowl.

Born: 2/14/73

Hometown: Mount Olive, MS

College: Alcorn State

NFL Draft: 1st Round, 1995

McNair Trivia: *At age 29, Steve became the fifth player with 18,000 career passing yards and 3,000 career rushing yards. Name the other four.*

ROGER STAUBACH

Ht: 6'3" Wt: 197 Pro Career: 1969–1979

Roger Staubach, who won the Heisman Trophy as a junior, was one of the most highly regarded players in the nation when he graduated in 1965. But thanks to a tour of duty with the Navy, which included a stint in the Vietnam War, Staubach did not join the Cowboys until 1969, and he wasn't a starter until 1971. That season, he was named Super Bowl VI MVP as he led Dallas to its first title. Staubach's penchant for late-game heroics earned him the nickname "Captain Comeback." He led the NFL in passing four times, and was selected to six Pro Bowls. Behind Staubach, the Cowboys were one of the NFL's most successful teams during the 1970s, winning 73 percent of their games.

Born: 2/5/42
Hometown: Cincinnati, OH
College: Navy
NFL Draft: 10th Round, 1964

Staubach Trivia: *Roger threw 8 touchdown passes to seven different receivers in Super Bowl play. What receiver had 2 touchdown catches?*

Answer: Butch Johnson

FRAN TARKENTON

Ht: 6'0" Wt: 190 Pro Career: 1961–1978

Fran Tarkenton retired in 1978 as the NFL career leader in passing yards, completions, and touchdown passes, not to mention rushing yards by a quarterback. Tarkenton was an instant success, passing for 250 yards and 4 touchdowns as the expansion Vikings defeated the Chicago Bears in Minnesota's first game. He played 18 seasons—13 with the Vikings, 5 with the Giants—and led Minnesota to three Super Bowls. An elusive scrambler, Tarkenton was the NFL's MVP in 1975, earned nine Pro Bowl berths, and retired with more than 50,000 total yards (47,003 passing and 3,674 rushing).

Born: 2/3/40
Hometown: Richmond, VA
College: Georgia
NFL Draft: 3rd Round, 1961

Tarkenton Trivia: *Fran was the Vikings' quarterback for three of their four Super Bowl appearances. Who was the starter in Super Bowl IV?*

MICHAEL VICK

Ht: *6'0"* **Wt:** *215* **Pro Career:** *2001–present*

Unstoppable. Unbelievable. Unreal. These are some of the words used to describe Michael Vick, who became one of the league's biggest stars in 2002, his first year as a starter. On December 1, Vick set an NFL mark for a quarterback by rushing for 173 yards, including a 46-yard touchdown scamper in overtime to beat the Vikings. With a nondescript supporting cast, Vick guided Atlanta to the playoffs, and then the Falcons stunned nearly everyone by becoming the first road team to win a postseason game at Green Bay. The scary part for opponents: Vick, just 22 in 2002, is only going to get better.

Born: *6/26/80*
Hometown: *Newport News, VA*
College: *Virginia Tech*
NFL Draft: *1st Round, 2001*

Vick Trivia: *What team traded the rights to the first pick of the 2001 NFL Draft to Atlanta?*

STEVE YOUNG

Ht: 6'2" Wt: 205 Pro Career: 1984–1999

Steve Young led the NFL in passer rating six times during a seven-year span (1991–97), and surpassed the 100-point mark six times in his career (next is Joe Montana with three). Young played two seasons in the USFL and two with the Tampa Bay Buccaneers before joining the 49ers and backing up Montana for four seasons. In eight seasons as a full-time starter (1991–98), he led the NFL in touchdown passes four times and ran for 33 scores. His 4,239 rushing yards rank second among all quarterbacks, and he's the NFL's all-time leader in passer rating and completion percentage.

Born: *10/11/61*
Hometown: *Salt Lake City, UT*
College: *Brigham Young*
NFL Draft: *1st Round, 1984*
   (Supplemental Draft)

Young Trivia: *For which United States Football League team did Steve play in 1984 and 1985?*

FREE SPIRITS

GEORGE BLANDA

Ht: 6'2" Wt: 215 Pro Career: 1949–1975

George Blanda played a record 26 seasons as a quarterback and kicker, during which he became pro football's all-time leading scorer. He captured headlines during a five-game stretch in 1970 when his last-minute touchdown passes or field goals led the Raiders to four victories and 1 tie—at the age of 43. Blanda passed for 236 touchdowns, including a record 36 for the 1961 Houston Oilers, and twice led the AFL in passing yards. In 1974, at the age of 47 and despite not having attempted a pass for two years, he became the oldest player to throw a touchdown pass with his 28-yard strike to Cliff Branch.

Born: 9/17/27
Hometown: Youngwood, PA
College: Kentucky
NFL Draft: 12th Round, 1949

Blanda Trivia: *Name the kicker who, in 2000, surpassed George's NFL-record total of 2,002 points.*

Answer: Gary Anderson

BRETT FAVRE

Ht: *6'2"* **Wt:** *225* **Pro Career:** *1991–present*

One day it will happen—Brett Favre will not start a game at quarterback. But he entered 2003 with 173 consecutive starts, shattering the previous record of 116. Favre is the only player with 11 consecutive 3,000-yard seasons, has been selected to seven Pro Bowls, passed for 30 touchdowns a record six times, and is the NFL's only three-time MVP (1995–97).

Originally drafted by Atlanta, the Packers traded for Favre in 1992. Favre replaced an injured Don Majkowski in the third game, and rallied the Packers from a 10-point fourth-quarter deficit to victory. He has started every game since.

Born: *10/10/69*
Hometown: *Gulfport, MS*
College: *Southern Mississippi*
NFL Draft: *2nd Round, 1991*

Favre Trivia: *Name the quarterback who started 116 consecutive games, the record streak that Brett broke.*

SONNY JURGENSEN

Ht: 5'11" Wt: 202 Pro Career: 1957–1974

Sonny Jurgensen was famous for staying in the pocket and delivering the ball the instant before being hit by a pass rusher. Though he was a backup when the Eagles won the 1960 NFL title and was a member of the 1972 Redskins team that won the NFC title, Jurgensen spent most of his career with mediocre teams. But he made those teams competitive with his arm, as he was the NFL's most prolific passer during the 1960s. He led the NFL in passing yards five times, including a record 3,723 yards in 1961. He also twice led the NFL in touchdown passes. Only Fran Tarkenton and Johnny Unitas had more passing yards and touchdown passes at the time of Jurgensen's retirement.

Born: 8/23/34
Hometown: Wilmington, NC
College: Duke
NFL Draft: 4th Round, 1957

Jurgensen Trivia: *When an injury sidelined Sonny in 1972, who played quarterback for the Redskins in Super Bowl VII?*

BOBBY LAYNE

Ht: **6'1"** *Wt:* **201** *Pro Career:* **1948–1962**

"Bobby Layne never lost a game. He sometimes ran out of time." That statement epitomizes Layne's career. A good ol' boy from Texas, Layne was a leader on the field and the life of the party off it. The Detroit Lions won their last three NFL titles with Layne during the 1950s. Traded to Pittsburgh in 1958, he helped guide the Steelers to their first winning season in nine years. In his last season, the Steelers' 9–5 record was the second best in franchise history. Layne retired with an NFL-record 196 touchdown passes, and was inducted into the Pro Football Hall Fame in 1967.

Born: **12/19/26**
Hometown: **Santa Ana, TX**
College: **Texas**
NFL Draft: **1st Round, 1948**

Layne Trivia: *What future Pro Football Hall of Fame quarterback did Bobby back up in his only season with the Chicago Bears, as a rookie in 1948?*

Answer: Sid Luckman

JIM MCMAHON

Ht: 6'1" Wt: 195 Pro Career: 1982–1996

Jim McMahon, who passed for 47 touchdowns as a junior at BYU, was selected with the fifth choice of the 1982 draft. He passed for only 100 career NFL touchdowns, but directed one of the NFL's most fabled teams—the Super Bowl XX champion Bears. He is remembered for sideline spats with coach Mike Ditka and for his colorful, outspoken personality, but he also led Chicago to five consecutive NFC Central titles. The reckless abandon with which he played caused him to sit out many games with injuries, but he posted 22 consecutive regular-season victories (1984–87), a streak unmatched in the modern era.

Born: *8/21/59*
Hometown: *Jersey City, NJ*
College: *Brigham Young*
NFL Draft: *1st Round, 1982*

McMahon Trivia: *Other than the Chicago Bears, name the five other teams for which Jim played at least one game.*

DON MEREDITH

Ht: 6'3" **Wt:** 210 **Pro Career:** 1960-68

"He has this charisma about him," the Rams' Merlin Olsen said of Don Meredith. "He's...a great player and leader....Meredith to me is what I want—and what I expect—an NFL quarterback to be." A two-time All-America pick at SMU, "Dandy Don" started out as a kid playing for his hometown team but ended up as the personification of the Cowboys. He led Dallas to the playoffs each of his last three seasons. Injuries ended his career at age 30, after which Meredith went on to an illustrious 12-year stint as a broadcaster on *NFL Monday Night Football*.

Born: 4/10/38
Hometown: Mount Vernon, TX
College: Southern Methodist
NFL Draft: 3rd Round, 1960

Meredith Trivia: *What two people were Don's main partners during his* NFL Monday Night Football *broadcasting career (1970–73, 1977–1984)?*

JOE NAMATH

In 1965, Joe Namath signed the richest contract in football history, a $400,000 deal, when the AFL's Jets outbid the NFL's St. Louis Cardinals. Playing in New York City, the charismatic bachelor with the cannon arm became "Broadway Joe," and a media darling was born. In 1967, Namath became the first player to pass for 4,000 yards in a season. The following year he guided the club to Super Bowl III, whereupon he "guaranteed" the Jets' upset of the Colts. Four knee surgeries curtailed his mobility and forced his premature retirement, but not before he had passed for 27,663 yards.

Born: 5/31/43
Hometown: Beaver Falls, PA
College: Alabama
NFL Draft: 1st Round, 1965

Namath Trivia: *After 12 seasons (1965–1976) with the New York Jets, Joe played for what team in his final season?*

KENNY STABLER

Ht: *6'3"* **Wt:** *215* **Pro Career:** *1970–1984*

With his long mane, facial hair, and late-night escapades, Ken Stabler was an ideal fit for the Raiders' rowdy, bad-boy image. But he also was the consummate field general. He was accurate with the short passing game, twice leading the NFL in completion percentage. But he also could throw deep, perfect for the club's "vertical" passing game. A winner at every level, he collected two high school titles and led Alabama to an undefeated season and NCAA title. Stabler guided Oakland to five consecutive AFC title games (1973–77), and he led the NFL with a 103.4 passer rating in 1976, when he guided Oakland to a 32–14 victory in Super Bowl XI.

Born: *12/25/45*
Hometown: *Foley, AL*
College: *Alabama*
NFL Draft: *2nd Round, 1968*

Stabler Trivia: *What nickname was bestowed upon Kenny, inspired by his ability to slither out of trouble?*

TRENDSETTERS

KEN ANDERSON

Ht: *6'2"* **Wt:** *212* **Pro Career:** *1971–1986*

Ken Anderson, the first quarterback to master the West Coast offense, set the standard: His 70.55 completion percentage in 1982 is an NFL record. Only Sammy Baugh and Steve Young have won more passing titles than Anderson (four), three times he led the league in lowest interception percentage. Anderson, who spent his entire career with the Bengals, played his best in the playoffs, registering the highest completion percentage (66.3) and third-best passer rating (93.5) in postseason history. In his lone Super Bowl appearance, Anderson passed for 300 yards and 2 touchdowns in XVI.

Born: *2/15/49*
Hometown: *Batavia, IL*
College: *Augustana (IL)*
NFL Draft: *3rd Round, 1971*

Anderson Trivia: *When Ken completed 20 consecutive passes in a January 1983 game, whose single-game record did he break?*

SAMMY BAUGH

Ht: 6'2" Wt: 182 Pro Career: 1937–1952

Sammy Baugh was the first great passer, appropriate for a player nicknamed Slingin' Sammy. He held virtually every passing record when he retired, and his six passing titles are matched only by Steve Young. He led the NFL in completion percentage seven times and passing yards four times. He joined the Redskins in 1937, their first season in Washington, and promptly guided them to the NFL title. A fantastic athlete, Baugh also led the NFL in punting four times (his 51.4-yard average in 1940 still is a record) and starred as a defensive back (he intercepted an NFL-high 11 passes in 1943).

Born: 3/17/14
Hometown: Temple, TX
College: Texas Christian
NFL Draft: 1st Round, 1937

Baugh Trivia: *Sammy was the only quarterback inducted as part of the charter class of the Pro Football Hall of Fame. What year did the Hall open?*

RANDALL CUNNINGHAM

Ht: *6'4"* **Wt:** *215* **Pro Career:** *1985–2001*

Randall Cunningham is the NFL's all-time rushing leader among quarterbacks with 4,928 yards. He struggled at first, getting sacked a then-record 72 times in 1986 with the Philadelphia Eagles, but he responded with four consecutive seasons of at least 20 touchdown passes and 500 rushing yards. In 1990, he finished ninth in the NFL with 942 rushing yards. Cunningham's best season was in 1998, when the 35-year-old, who had been out of football two years earlier, led the Minnesota Vikings to a record-tying 15–1 record and posted career highs in touchdown passes (34) and passer rating (an NFL-high 106.0).

Born: *3/27/63*
Hometown: **Santa Barbara, CA**
College: **Nevada-Las Vegas**
NFL Draft: **2nd Round, 1985**

Cunningham Trivia: *For what network did Randall serve as a studio analyst during his one-year hiatus from football in 1996?*

73

LEN DAWSON

Ht: *6'0"* **Wt:** *190* **Pro Career:** *1957–1975*

Len Dawson was the winningest quarterback in AFL history. Dawson, who had been selected ahead of Jim Brown in the 1957 NFL Draft, attempted just 45 passes in five seasons before joining the AFL's Dallas Texans in 1962. Given a starting role, Dawson led the league in touchdown passes his first season and guided Dallas to the AFL title. The Texans moved to Kansas City in 1963, and the Chiefs won two more AFL titles and Super Bowl IV. Coach Hank Stram said Dawson "was the most accurate passer in pro football." The numbers bear that out—he led the league in completion percentage a record eight times.

Born: *6/20/35*
Hometown: *Alliance, OH*
College: *Purdue*
NFL Draft: *1st Round, 1957*

Dawson Trivia: *What two NFL teams did Len play for before joining the AFL's Dallas Texans in 1962?*

OTTO GRAHAM

Ht: *6'1"* **Wt:** *196* **Pro Career:** *1946–1955*

If the number of championship games played is the best measure of a quarterback's greatness, Otto Graham is the best quarterback of all time. Graham guided the Browns to all four AAFC titles (1946–49). When the Browns joined the NFL in 1950, he led the club to the championship game each of the next six seasons (1950–55), winning three times. He ran for 3 scores and passed for 3 in the 1954 NFL Championship Game. Graham, who earned all-league honors in 9 of his 10 seasons, capped his career by accounting for 4 touchdowns in the Browns' 38–14 victory in the 1955 NFL title game.

Born: *12/6/21*
Hometown: *Waukegan, IL*
College: *Northwestern*
NFL Draft: *1st Round, 1944*

Graham Trivia: *The Cleveland Browns have won four NFL titles, three of which came during Otto's era. In what year did they win their other title?*

JAMES HARRIS

Ht: *6'4"* **Wt:** *210* **Pro Career:** *1969–1979*

Before Donovan McNabb and Doug Williams, there was James Harris, the first African-American quarterback to become a full-time starter. Harris, who was drafted by the Bills in 1969, joined Los Angeles four years later. He guided the Rams to a 1974 playoff victory (in the first postseason start by a black quarterback), and was the NFC passing leader in 1976. As Baltimore's pro personnel director from 1997-2002, he helped put together the Ravens' team that won Super Bowl XXXV. In 2003, the Jaguars named Harris their vice president of player personnel.

Born: *7/20/47*
Hometown: *Monroe, LA*
College: *Grambling State*
NFL Draft: *8th Round, 1969*

Harris Trivia: *James played with three teams during his 10-year NFL career. After playing for the Bills and Rams, what team did James play for from 1977-79?*

79

SID LUCKMAN

Ht: 6'0" Wt: 197 Pro Career: 1939–1950

As the NFL's first great T-formation quarterback, Sid Luckman helped revolutionize football. In that formation, the Bears' offense closely resembled today's look, with two wide receivers, men in motion, and a tight end. Behind Luckman, the Bears shattered their own scoring record in 1939, and the T-formation became the NFL standard after he and the Bears handed the Redskins a 73–0 defeat in the 1940 title game. He passed for 286 yards and 5 touchdowns in the 1943 NFL Championship Game, the third of four championships won by the Bears in Luckman's 12 seasons.

Born: 11/21/16
Hometown: Brooklyn, NY
College: Columbia
NFL Draft: 1st Round, 1939

Luckman Trivia: *Sid's Bears defeated the Redskins in two NFL Championship Games. What team did Chicago defeat to win its other two titles during the 1940s?*

Y.A. TITTLE

Ht: *6'0"* **Wt:** *192* **Pro Career:** *1948–1964*

Y.A. Tittle was one of the first quarterbacks to have a career renaissance after age 35. A first-round pick of Detroit in 1948, he opted for the AAFC's Baltimore Colts, for whom he played three seasons, including the club's first year in the NFL. With the 49ers, Tittle led San Francisco to one playoff appearance in 10 seasons. He joined the Giants in 1961, and at age 36 in 1962, passed for a career-high 3,224 yards. He added a personal-best 36 touchdown passes in 1963, and led the Giants to the 1962 and 1963 title games. He retired as the all-time leader in passing yards and touchdowns.

Born: *10/24/26*
Hometown: *Marshall, TX*
College: *Louisiana State*
NFL Draft: *1st Round, 1948*

Tittle Trivia: *Name the 49ers' receiver who was nicknamed "Alley Oop" because of his knack for catching Y.A.'s high lofted passes.*

JOHNNY UNITAS

Ht: **6'1"** *Wt:* **194** *Pro Career:* **1956–1973**

The magic number is 47. That's how many consecutive games in which Johnny U. threw a touchdown pass. No one has come within a season of breaking Unitas' immortal feat. Cut by the 1955 Steelers, he played semi-pro ball before signing with the Colts. An injury to starter George Shaw four games into the 1956 season thrust Unitas into the lineup, where he remained until 1972. Unitas guided the Colts to the game-tying and winning drives in the "greatest game ever played," the 1958 NFL Championship Game. He earned 10 Pro Bowl selections, and in 2000, he was selected quarterback on the NFL's All-Time Team.

Born: **5/7/33**
Hometown: **Pittsburgh, PA**
College: **Louisville**
NFL Draft: **9th Round, 1955**

Unitas Trivia: *Johnny's only Super Bowl touchdown pass came in game V. What Pro Football Hall of Fame tight end caught that pass?*

NORM VAN BROCKLIN

Ht: 6'1" Wt: 190 Pro Career: 1949–1960

After joining the Rams in 1949, Norm Van Brocklin shared quarterback duties with Bob Waterfield for four seasons. Together, they guided the high-scoring Rams to four playoff appearances, and Van Brocklin won the passing title in 1950, 1952, and 1954. In 1951, Van Brocklin passed for 554 yards (a single-game record that still stands) as the Rams defeated the New York Yanks. "The Dutchman" joined a downtrodden Eagles team in 1958 and turned the team into a winner. He went out on top, as he guided the Eagles to the 1960 NFL title in his final game. He entered the Pro Football Hall of Fame in 1971.

Born: 3/15/26
Hometown: Eagle Butte, SD
College: Oregon
NFL Draft: 4th Round, 1949

Van Brocklin Trivia: *Norm coached the Minnesota Vikings for six seasons and what other NFL team for seven years?*

BOB WATERFIELD

Ht: *6'1"* **Wt:** *200* **Pro Career:** *1945–1952*

The Cleveland Rams did not post a winning record during their first eight seasons, but thanks to Bob Waterfield, they enjoyed a reversal of fortune in 1945, when the rookie guided the Rams to the NFL title. The good fortune continued after the Rams moved to Los Angeles in 1946. Waterfield shared time with Norm Van Brocklin, and the duo posted record-setting numbers. The Rams led the NFL in scoring from 1950–52, including a record average of 38.8 points per game in 1950. Waterfield led the NFL in passing in 1946 and 1951, when the Rams won another NFL title.

Born: *7/26/20*
Hometown: *Elmira, NY*
College: *UCLA*
NFL Draft: *3rd Round, 1944*

Waterfield Trivia: *Name the Hollywood actress who was married to Bob from 1943–1967.*

Answer: Jane Russell

CLASSIC PASSERS

DREW BLEDSOE

Ht: *6'5"* **Wt:** *240* **Pro Career:** *1993–present*

Drew Bledsoe, the first pick of the 1993 draft, began his career with a Patriots team that had won a total of nine games the previous three years. He led New England to the playoffs in his second season, and in 1996, Bledsoe guided the team to Super Bowl XXXI. Along the way, he set club records for attempts, completions, and yards. Following an injury in 2001, the Patriots traded him to Buffalo. In his first season with the Bills, Drew passed for a club-record 4,359 yards, and Buffalo went 8–8, a five-game improvement from 2001. Just 31 years old, Drew ranks sixteenth in career passing yards.

Born: *2/14/72*
Hometown: *Ellensburg, WA*
College: *Washington State*
NFL Draft: *1st Round, 1993*

Bledsoe Trivia: *Drew, at the age of 23, became the youngest player to reach 10,000 passing yards. Whose record did he break?*

TOM BRADY

Ht: 6'4" Wt: 220 Pro Career: 2000-present

The 2001 season must have seemed like a dream to Tom Brady. Thrust into the lineup following an injury to Drew Bledsoe, Brady guided the Patriots to 14 victories in 17 games, including a 20–17 win in Super Bowl XXXVI. He led a fourth-quarter comeback in a snowstorm against Oakland during the playoffs, and the game-winning drive in the final 1:21 of the Super Bowl. Not only is Brady the youngest quarterback (24 years, 184 days) to win a Super Bowl, he also attempted 162 passes before being intercepted, the longest such streak to begin an NFL career. In 2002, he led the NFL with 28 scoring passes.

Born: 8/3/77
Hometown: San Mateo, CA
College: Michigan
NFL Draft: 6th Round, 2000

Brady Trivia: *In 2001, Tom became the fifth player to complete at least 70 percent of his passes in four consecutive games. Name the others.*

BOOMER ESIASON

Ht: *6'5"* **Wt:** *224* **Pro Career:** *1984–1997*

The most prolific left-handed quarterback in NFL history, Boomer Esiason ranks eleventh in both career passing yards and touchdowns. He passed for at least 3,000 yards in each of his first six seasons (1985–1990) as a starter for the Bengals. His best season was in 1988, when he led the NFL in passer rating, earned league MVP honors, and guided the Bengals to Super Bowl XXIII. His ability to decipher coverages allowed him to pick apart defenses. In his final season, he completed 63 percent of his passes and posted a 13:2 touchdown-to-interception ratio.

Born: *4/17/61*
Hometown: *West Islip, NY*
College: *Maryland*
NFL Draft: *2nd Round, 1984*

Esiason Trivia: *For what team was Boomer playing in 1996, when he passed for 522 yards, the third-highest single-game mark in NFL history?*

DAN FOUTS

Ht: 6'3" Wt: 204 Pro Career: 1973–1987

When Don Coryell was named the Chargers' coach in 1978, he saw a strong-armed quarterback and a plethora of quality receivers. He took full advantage of the arsenal. Dan Fouts was the pilot of the Chargers' "Air Coryell" offense, and his numbers are among the best in NFL history. He is the only player to lead the league in passing yards in four consecutive seasons (1979–1982). He was the first player with eight 300-yard passing games (1980) in a season. At the time of his retirement, Fouts held the NFL record for career 300-yard games (51) and ranked second in career passing yards.

Born: 6/10/51
Hometown: San Francisco, CA
College: Oregon
NFL Draft: 3rd Round, 1973

Fouts Trivia: *As a child, Dan was a ball boy and his father was a radio announcer for which NFL team?*

Answer: San Francisco 49ers

JOHN HADL

Ht: 6'1" Wt: 214 Pro Career: 1962–1977

Chargers coach Sid Gillman loved to pass the ball, and John Hadl was more than willing to do his bidding. Hadl passed for at least 2,000 yards in 10 consecutive seasons, and registered seven seasons with at least 20 touchdown passes. He led the league in both passing yards and touchdown passes in 1968 and again in 1971. He is remembered as one of the best deep-ball passers in pro football history. Hadl appeared in six AFL All-Star Games, and never missed a game during his 16-year career. When he retired, he ranked third in career passing yards and fourth in touchdown passes on the NFL's all-time lists.

Born: 2/15/40
Hometown: Lawrence, KS
College: Kansas
NFL Draft: 3rd Round, 1962

Hadl Trivia: *Fifty-six of John Hadl's touchdown passes were caught by what Pro Football Hall of Fame receiver?*

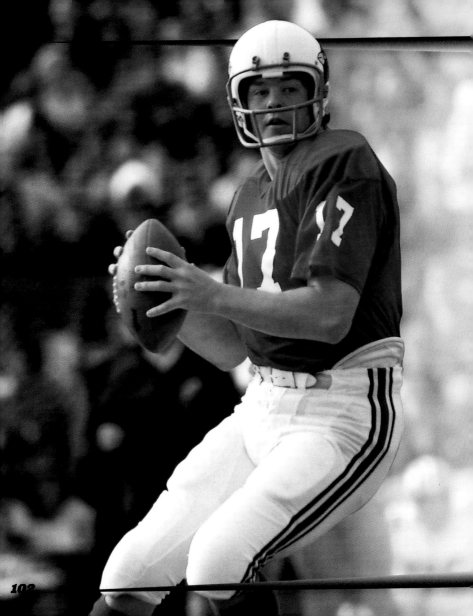

JIM HART

Ht: 6'1" Wt: 215 Pro Career: 1966–1984

An undrafted rookie in 1966, Jim Hart got his chance the following season when Charley Johnson was activated for military duty. Hart made the most of it, passing for 3,008 yards and 19 touchdowns to claim the position, a spot he would not relinquish for 15 seasons. When Hart guided the Cardinals to playoff berths in 1974 and 1975, it ended a playoff dry spell that had spanned 26 years. He passed for at least 2,000 yards in eight consecutive seasons, was selected to four Pro Bowls, and his 34,665 career passing yards ranked third in history when he retired.

Born: 4/29/44
Hometown: Evanston, IL
College: Southern Illinois
NFL Draft: Free Agent

Hart Trivia: *After 17 seasons in St. Louis, for what team did Jim finish his career, with 7 pass attempts in two games during the 1984 season?*

JIM KELLY

Ht: 6'3" Wt: 217 Pro Career: 1984–1996

Jim Kelly led the Bills to eight postseason berths, including four consecutive Super Bowls, during his 11 seasons in Buffalo. Selected with the fourteenth pick in the 1983 NFL Draft, Kelly spurned the Bills and played two seasons in the USFL, passing for 83 touchdowns. In 1986, he joined the Bills, who had won just four games during the previous two seasons. With Kelly they reached the playoffs in 1988. He averaged nearly 3,100 passing yards a season with the Bills, and led the NFL in passer rating in 1990 and scoring passes in 1991. In 2002, he entered the Pro Football Hall of Fame.

Born: *2/14/60*
Hometown: *Pittsburgh, PA*
College: *Miami*
NFL Draft: *1st Round, 1983*

Kelly Trivia: *Jim chose the University of Miami because Penn State coach Joe Paterno wanted him to switch to what position?*

PEYTON MANNING

Ht: 6'5" Wt: 230 Pro Career: 1998–present

Peyton Manning, the first overall pick of the 1998 NFL Draft, is the first player in NFL history to post four consecutive 4,000-yard passing seasons. Only Dan Marino reached 20,000 career passing yards in fewer games. He led the Colts to the playoffs three times in his first four seasons, matching the most successful four-year run in club history. In addition, Manning began his career with 80 consecutive starts, the longest such streak for a quarterback in NFL history. Manning, who has been selected to play in three Pro Bowls, also set NFL rookie records for passing yards and scoring passes.

Born: 3/24/76
Hometown: New Orleans, LA
College: Tennessee
NFL Draft: 1st Round, 1998

Manning Trivia: *Peyton's dad, Archie, passed for nearly 24,000 yards while in the NFL. With what team did he spend the majority of his career?*

DAN MARINO

Ht: 6'4" Wt: 218 Pro Career: 1983–1999

Dan Marino owns nearly every NFL career passing record. He is the leader in passing yards (nearly 10,000 more than second place) and touchdown passes (78 more than second). He posted the NFL's lone 5,000-yard season when he passed for 5,084 yards in 1984, just his second year. That season, Marino became the youngest quarterback to start a Super Bowl. His 21 career 4-touchdown games are a record, as are his 13 career 400-yard games. With 48 touchdown passes in 1984 and 44 in 1986, he owns the top two single-season marks. His 147 victories rank second only to John Elway.

Born: 9/15/61
Hometown: Pittsburgh, PA
College: Pittsburgh
NFL Draft: 1st Round, 1983

Marino Trivia: *Whom did Dan replace at quarterback for the Dolphins during the 1983 season to become the full-time starter?*

WARREN MOON

Ht: *6'3"* **Wt:** *212* **Pro Career:** *1978–2000*

Warren Moon began his pro career in the Canadian Football League, where he played six seasons with the Edmonton Eskimos and won Grey Cup titles each of his last five years. He signed with Houston in 1984 to start a 17-year NFL career. Moon guided the Oilers to seven consecutive postseason appearances (1987–1993), twice leading the NFL in passing yards (1990 and 1991). He ranked third in NFL history in passing yards when he retired, and his 527 yards in a 1990 game are the most in the last 50 years. Including his CFL totals, his 435 scoring passes and 70,553 passing yards are both pro records.

Born: *11/18/56*
Hometown: *Los Angeles, CA*
College: *Washington*
NFL Draft: *Free Agent*

Moon Trivia: *How old was Warren when he became the oldest player to win the Pro Bowl player of the game award?*

PHIL SIMMS

Ht: 6'3" Wt: 216 Pro Career: 1979–1993

The Giants surprised everyone when they picked Phil Simms out of Morehead State in the first round of the 1979 draft. Two years later, however, he helped New York reach the playoffs for the first time since 1963. Injuries limited Simms to a total of two games in 1982 and 1983. Simms recovered, and in 1986, he led the Giants to Super Bowl XXI, where he played a near-perfect game (22 of 25 pass attempts for a record 88.0 completion percentage) as the Giants routed the Broncos. Simms missed the Giants' Super Bowl XXV victory with an injury, but posted a 92.7 passer rating during the club's 13–3 season.

Born: 11/3/54
Hometown: Lebanon, KY
College: Morehead State
NFL Draft: 1st Round, 1979

Simms Trivia: *Name the quarterback who replaced Phil late in the 1990 season and for the postseason run capped by Super Bowl XXV.*

KURT WARNER

Ht: 6'2" Wt: 220 Pro Career: 1995–present

Warner guided the Rams to two Super Bowls, including victory in XXXIV, in his first three seasons as a starter. He passed for 41 touchdowns in 1999 and 36 in 2001 to win league MVP honors each year. But success did not come overnight for Warner. He went to the Packers' training camp in 1994 behind Brett Favre, Ty Detmer, and Mark Brunell and was cut.

Warner played three seasons in the Arena League and led NFL Europe in passing yards and touchdowns in spring of 1998. He was a third-string quarterback with the Rams that year, but by 1999 he was leading St. Louis to the Super Bowl.

Born: 6/22/71
Hometown: Burlington, IA
College: Northern Iowa
NFL Draft: Free Agent

Warner Trivia: *Kurt passed for 10,486 yards and 183 touchdowns in three seasons (1995–97) in the Arena League. For what team did he play?*

STATISTICS

TROY AIKMAN (for more information, see pages 8–9)

Year	Team	G	Att	Comp	Pct	Yds	YPA	TD	Int	Rating	Rushing		
											Att	Yds	TD
1989	Dallas	11	293	155	52.9	1,749	5.97	9	18	55.7	38	302	0
1990	Dallas	15	399	226	56.6	2,579	6.46	11	18	66.6	40	172	1
1991	Dallas	12	363	237	65.3	2,754	7.59	11	10	86.7	16	5	1
1992	Dallas	16	473	302	63.8	3,445	7.28	23	14	89.5	37	105	1
1993	Dallas	14	392	271	69.1*	3,100	7.91	15	6	99.0	32	125	0
1994	Dallas	14	361	233	64.5	2,676	7.41	13	12	84.9	30	62	1
1995	Dallas	16	432	280	64.8	3,304	7.65	16	7	93.6	21	32	1
1996	Dallas	15	465	296	63.7	3,126	6.72	12	13	80.1	35	42	1
1997	Dallas	16	518	292	56.4	3,283	6.34	19	12	78.0	25	79	0
1998	Dallas	11	315	187	59.4	2,330	7.40	12	5	88.5	22	69	2
1999	Dallas	11	442	263	59.5	2,964	6.71	17	12	81.1	21	10	1
2000	Dallas	11	262	156	59.5	1,632	6.23	7	14	64.3	10	13	0
Totals		**165**	**4,715**	**2,898**	**61.5**	**32,942**	**6.99**	**165**	**141**	**81.6**	**327**	**1,016**	**9**

*Led league

Transactions
- Selected by Dallas Cowboys in the first round (first pick overall) of the 1989 NFL Draft;
- On injured reserve with shoulder injury (December 28–end of 1990 season).

Noteworthy
- Selected to six Pro Bowls (following 1991–1996 seasons);
- Starting quarterback for Cowboys' Super Bowl XXVII, XXVIII, and XXX victories;
- Completed 22 of 30 passes for 273 yards and 4 touchdowns and won MVP award in XXVII;
- Completed 19 of 27 passes for 207 yards in XXVIII;
- Completed 15 of 23 passes for 209 yards and 1 touchdown in XXX;
- Most accurate passer in Super Bowl history (70 percent completion rate);
- Completed second-longest pass in postseason history (94 yards to Alvin Harper in 1994 divisional playoff);
- Third-most accurate passer in postseason history (63 percent completion rate);
- Tied for third in postseason history with four games of 300 or more passing yards;
- Cowboys career leader in completions, passing yards, completion percentage, and touchdowns;
- Cowboys season leader in completion percentage (1993);
- First in club history with 16 consecutive games with a touchdown pass (1993–94);
- First in club history with 216 consecutive passes without interception (1999);
- First in club history for lowest percentage of passes intercepted in a season (1.53 in 1993) and a career (2.99);
- Posted 90 regular-season victories during the 1990s, the most by any quarterback in any decade;
- Family moved to Henryetta, Oklahoma when Troy was 12, and he left his mark on the town: Aikman had high school jersey retired, was named to the Oklahoma High School Football All-Time Team, and Henryetta (population 6,000) named a street after him.

KEN ANDERSON (for more information, see pages 68–69)

YEAR	TEAM	G	ATT	COMP	PCT	YDS	YPA	TD	INT	RATING	RUSHING ATT	YDS	TD
1971	Cincinnati	11	131	72	55.0	777	5.93	5	4	72.6	22	125	1
1972	Cincinnati	13	301	171	56.8	1,918	6.37	7	7	74.0	22	94	3
1973	Cincinnati	14	329	179	54.4	2,428	7.38	18	12	81.2	26	97	0
1974	Cincinnati	13	328	213*	64.9*	2,667*	8.13*	18	10	95.7*	43	314	2
1975	Cincinnati	13	377	228	60.5	3,169*	8.41	21	11	93.9*	49	188	2
1976	Cincinnati	14	338	179	53.0	2,367	7.00	19	14	76.9	31	134	1
1977	Cincinnati	14	323	166	51.4	2,145	6.64	11	11	69.7	26	128	2
1978	Cincinnati	12	319	173	54.2	2,219	6.96	10	22	58.0	29	167	1
1979	Cincinnati	15	339	189	55.8	2,340	6.90	16	10	80.7	28	235	2
1980	Cincinnati	13	275	166	60.4	1,778	6.47	6	13	66.9	16	122	0
1981	Cincinnati	16	479	300	62.6	3,754	7.84	29	10	98.4*	46	320	1
1982	Cincinnati	9	309	218*	70.6*	2,495	8.07	12	9	95.3*	25	85	4
1983	Cincinnati	13	297	198	66.7*	2,333	7.86	12	13	85.6	22	147	1
1984	Cincinnati	11	275	175	63.6	2,107	7.66	10	12	81.0	11	64	0
1985	Cincinnati	3	32	16	50.0	170	5.31	2	0	86.7	1	0	0
1986	Cincinnati	8	23	11	47.8	171	7.43	1	2	51.2	0	0	0
Totals		**192**	**4,475**	**2,654**	**59.3**	**32,838**	**7.34**	**197**	**160**	**81.9**	**397**	**2,220**	**20**

*Led league

Transactions
• Selected by Cincinnati Bengals in the third round (67th pick overall) of the 1971 NFL Draft.

Noteworthy
• Selected to play in four Pro Bowls (following 1975, 1976, 1981, and 1982 seasons);
• 1981 NFL player of the year;
• In 1981, guided Bengals to AFC's best record (12–4) and berth in Super Bowl XVI;
• Completed 25 of 34 passes for 300 yards and 2 touchdowns in Super Bowl XVI;
• Bengals also reached the playoffs in 1973, 1975, and 1982;
• Ranks third in NFL history for postseason passer rating (93.5);
• Holds NFL record for highest completion percentage in a season (70.55 in 1982).
• Completed then-NFL-record 20 consecutive passes in a game (vs. Houston, Jan. 2, 1983);
• Completed then-NFL-record 90.9 percent of his passes in a game (20 of 22 vs. Pittsburgh, Nov. 10, 1974);
• Tied for second in NFL history for most seasons with the lowest percentage passes intercepted (3 in 1972, 1981–82);
• Holds club records for passing yards, completions, touchdown passes, and service (16 seasons);
• Served as Bengals assisant coach since 1993;
• Pro Football Hall of Fame coach Bill Walsh, who was an assistant coach in Cincinnati (1968–1975): "Anderson never has received the credit he deserves…Few players had the talent, the understanding of the game, and the intuitive feeling Ken did."

SAMMY BAUGH (for more information, see pages 70–71)

Year	Team	G	Att	Comp	Pct	Yds	YPA	TD	Int	Rating	Rushing Att	Yds	TD
1937	Washington	11	171*	81*	47.4	1,127*	6.59	8	14	50.5*	86	240	1
1938	Washington	9	128	63	49.2	853	6.66	5	11	48.1	21	35	0
1939	Washington	9	96	53	55.2	518	5.40	6	9	52.3	14	46	0
1940	Washington	11	177	111	62.7*	1,367*	7.72	12*	10	85.6*	20	16	0
1941	Washington	11	193	106	54.9	1,236	6.40	10	19	52.2	27	14	0
1942	Washington	11	225	132	58.7*	1,524	6.77	16	11	82.5	20	61	1
1943	Washington	10	239*	133*	55.6*	1,754	7.34	23	19	78.0*	19	-43	0
1944	Washington	8	146	82	56.2	849	5.82	4	8	59.4	19	-38	0
1945	Washington	8	182	128*	70.3*	1,669	9.17	11	4	109.9*	19	-71	0
1946	Washington	11	161	87	54.0	1,163	7.22	8	17	54.2	18	-76	1
1947	Washington	12	354*	210*	59.3*	2,938*	8.30	25*	15	92.0*	25	47	2
1948	Washington	12	315*	185*	58.7*	2,599*	8.25	22	23	78.3	4	4	1
1949	Washington	12	255	145	56.9*	1,903	7.46	18	14	81.2*	13	67	2
1950	Washington	11	166	90	54.2	1,130	6.81	10	11	68.1	7	27	1
1951	Washington	12	154	67	43.5	1,104	7.17	7	17	43.8	11	-5	0
1952	Washington	7	33	20	60.6	152	4.61	2	1	79.4	1	1	0
Totals		**165**	**2,995**	**1,693**	**56.5**	**21,886**	**7.31**	**187**	**203**	**72.2**	**324**	**325**	**9**

*Led league

Transactions
- Selected by Boston Redskins in the first round (sixth pick overall) of the 1937 NFL Draft;
- Redskins moved from Boston to Washington prior to 1937 season.

Noteworthy
- Inducted into Pro Football Hall of Fame as part of Charter Class of 1963;
- Selected to five Pro Bowls (following 1938–41 and 1952 seasons. The Pro Bowl was not played for the 1943–49 seasons);
- Also punted 338 times for 15,245 yards for a 45.1-yard average;
- Scored 1 extra point by rushing, caught 1 pass for 0 yards, returned 11 punts for 99 yards, and intercepted 31 passes for 491 yards in his career;
- NFL all-time leader in: most seasons leading league in passing (6); most seasons lowest percentage passes intercepted, career (5 in 1940, 1942, 1944, 1945, 1947); highest average yardage gain, game (18.58 in 24 attempts for 446 yards, Oct. 31, 1948); most consecutive seasons leading league in punting (4 from 1940–43); highest punting average, career (45.10); highest punting average, season (51.4 in 1940).
- Shares NFL record for: most interceptions in a game (4 on Nov. 14, 1943); most seasons leading league in punting (4 from 1940–43);
- His uniform number 33 was retired by the Redskins;
- Slingin' Sammy's 81 completions his rookie season set an NFL record as he helped revolutionize the passing game.

GEORGE BLANDA (for more information, see pages 50–51)

Year	Team	G	Att	Comp	Pct	Yds	YPA	TD	Int	Rating	Rushing Att	Yds	TD
1949	Chicago Bears	12	21	9	42.9	197	9.38	0	5	37.3	2	9	1
1950	Baltimore Colts	1	0	0	—	0	—	0	0	—	0	0	0
1950	Chicago Bears	11	1	0	0.0	0	0.00	0	0	39.6	0	0	0
1951	Chicago Bears	12	0	0	—	0	—	0	0	—	0	0	0
1952	Chicago Bears	12	131	47	35.9	664	5.07	8	11	38.5	20	104	1
1953	Chicago Bears	12	362*	169*	46.7	2,164	5.98	14	23	52.3	24	62	0
1954	Chicago Bears	8	281	131	46.6	1,929	6.86	15	17	62.1	19	41	0
1955	Chicago Bears	12	97	42	43.3	459	4.73	4	7	41.6	15	54	2
1956	Chicago Bears	12	69	37	53.6	439	6.36	7	4	82.9	6	47	0
1957	Chicago Bears	12	19	8	42.1	65	3.42	0	3	11.8	5	-5	1
1958	Chicago Bears	12	7	2	28.6	19	2.71	0	0	39.6	0	0	0
1959						OUT OF FOOTBALL							
1960	Houston Oilers	14	363	169	46.6	2,413	6.65	24	22	65.4	16	16	4
1961	Houston Oilers	14	362	187	51.7	3,330*	9.20*	36*	22	91.3*	7	12	0
1962	Houston Oilers	14	418	197	47.1	2,810	6.72	27	42*	51.3	3	6	0
1963	Houston Oilers	14	423*	224*	53.0	3,003*	7.10	24	25	70.1	4	1	0
1964	Houston Oilers	14	505*	262*	51.9	3,287	6.51	17	27	61.4	4	-2	0
1965	Houston Oilers	14	442*	186*	42.1	2,542	5.75	20	30	47.9	4	-6	0
1966	Houston Oilers	14	271	122	45.0	1,764	6.51	17	21	55.3	3	1	0
1967	Oakland	14	38	15	39.5	285	7.50	3	3	59.6	0	0	0
1968	Oakland	14	49	30	61.2	522	10.65	6	2	120.1	0	0	0
1969	Oakland	14	13	6	46.2	73	5.62	2	1	71.5	1	0	0
1970	Oakland	14	55	29	52.7	461	8.38	6	5	79.4	2	4	0
1971	Oakland	14	58	32	55.2	378	6.52	4	6	58.6	0	0	0
1972	Oakland	14	15	5	33.3	77	5.13	1	0	73.5	0	0	0
1973	Oakland	14	0	0	—	0	—	0	0	—	0	0	0
1974	Oakland	14	4	1	25.0	28	7.00	1	0	95.8	0	0	0
1975	Oakland	14	3	1	33.3	11	3.67	0	1	5.6	0	0	0
Totals		**340**	**4,007**	**1,911**	**47.7**	**26,920**	**6.72**	**236**	**277***	**60.6**	**135**	**2,344**	**9**

Led league

Transactions
• Selected by Bears in the twelfth round (119th pick overall) of the 1949 NFL Draft;
• Traded by Bears to Baltimore Colts for guard Dick Barwegan (1950);
• Released by Colts, re-signed by Chicago Bears (September 1950);
• Released by Bears (1959), signed by Houston Oilers (1960);
• Released by Oilers, claimed off waivers by Oakland Raiders (May 1967).

Noteworthy
• Inducted into Pro Football Hall of Fame in 1981;
• Selected to play in four AFL All-Star Games (following 1961–63 and 1967 seasons);
• NFL all-time leader in: seasons played (26); games played (340); and extra points (943).

DREW BLEDSOE (for more information, see pages 92–93)

YEAR	TEAM	G	ATT	COMP	PCT	YDS	YPA	TD	INT	RATING	RUSHING ATT	YDS	TD
1993	New England	13	429	214	49.9	2,494	5.81	15	15	65.0	32	82	0
1994	New England	16	691*	400*	57.9	4,555*	6.59	25	27*	73.6	44	40	0
1995	New England	15	636*	323	50.8	3,507	5.51	13	16	63.7	20	28	0
1996	New England	16	623*	373*	59.9	4,086	6.56	27	15	83.7	24	27	0
1997	New England	16	522	314	60.2	3,706	7.10	28	15	87.7	28	55	0
1998	New England	14	481	263	54.7	3,633	7.55	20	14	80.9	28	44	0
1999	New England	16	539	305	56.6	3,985	7.39	19	21	75.6	42	101	0
2000	New England	16	531	312	58.8	3,291	6.20	17	13	77.3	47	158	2
2001	New England	2	66	40	60.6	400	6.06	2	2	75.3	5	18	0
2002	Buffalo	16	610	375	61.5	4,359	7.15	24	15	86.0	27	67	2
Totals		**140**	**5,128**	**2,919**	**56.9**	**34,016**	**6.63**	**190**	**153**	**77.1**	**297**	**620**	**4**

*Led league

Transactions
- Selected after junior season by New England Patriots in the first round (first pick overall) of the 1993 NFL Draft;
- Traded by Patriots to Buffalo Bills for first-round pick in 2003 NFL Draft (April 21, 2002).

Noteworthy
- Selected to four Pro Bowls (following 1994, 1996, 1997, and 2002 seasons);
- Starting quarterback for the Patriots in Super Bowl XXXI;
- Completed 25 of 48 passes for 253 yards and 2 touchdowns in XXXI;
- Holds NFL mark for passing touchdowns in overtime (4)—Terry Bradshaw (3) and Dan Fouts, Warren Moon (2), and Brian Sipe (2) are the only others with more than 1 overtime TD pass;
- NFL all-time leader for pass attempts in a season (691) and game (70 vs. Minnesota, Nov. 13, 1994);
- NFL all-time leader for completions in a game (45 vs. Minnesota, Nov. 13, 1994);
- In 1998, became first player in NFL history to complete game-winning touchdown passes in the final 30 seconds of consecutive games (against Miami, Nov. 23, 1998, and Buffalo, Nov. 29, 1998);
- Guided Patriots to their fourth postseason appearance in five years in 1998…after the Patriots reached the playoffs just six times in the 33 years prior to Bledsoe's arrival in New England;
- Missed majority of 2001 season because of chest injury;
- Entered 2001 AFC Championship Game late in second quarter and completed a touchdown pass as the Patriots defeated Pittsburgh and reached Super Bowl XXXVI;
- In his first season in Buffalo, set club season records for passing yards, completions, attempts, 300-yard games (7); and most consecutive passes without an interception (175);
- Set Bills single-game record for passing yards (463 at Minnesota, Sept. 15, 2002);
- When the Bills traded for Bledsoe, every Buffalo television station interrupted its their afternoon programming to broadcast Bledsoe's first press conference with the team.

TERRY BRADSHAW (for more information, see pages 10–11)

YEAR	TEAM	G	ATT	COMP	PCT	YDS	YPA	TD	INT	RATING	RUSHING ATT	YDS	TD
1970	Pittsburgh	13	218	83	38.1	1,410	6.47	6	24	30.4	32	233	1
1971	Pittsburgh	14	373	203	54.4	2,259	6.06	13	22	59.7	53	247	5
1972	Pittsburgh	14	308	147	47.7	1,887	6.13	12	12	64.1	58	346	7
1973	Pittsburgh	10	180	89	49.4	1,183	6.57	10	15	54.5	34	145	3
1974	Pittsburgh	8	148	67	45.3	785	5.30	7	8	55.2	34	224	2
1975	Pittsburgh	14	286	165	57.7	2,055	7.19	18	9	88.0	35	210	3
1976	Pittsburgh	10	192	92	47.9	1,177	6.13	10	9	65.4	31	219	3
1977	Pittsburgh	14	314	162	51.6	2,523	8.04*	17	19	71.4	31	171	3
1978	Pittsburgh	16	368	207	56.3	2,915	7.92*	28*	20	84.7	32	93	1
1979	Pittsburgh	16	472	259	54.9	3,724	7.89	26	25	77.0	21	83	0
1980	Pittsburgh	15	424	218	51.4	3,339	7.88	24	22	75.0	36	111	2
1981	Pittsburgh	14	370	201	54.3	2,887	7.80	22	14	83.9	38	162	2
1982	Pittsburgh	9	240	127	52.9	1,768	7.37	17*	11	81.4	8	10	2
1983	Pittsburgh	1	8	5	62.5	77	9.63	2	0	133.9	1	3	0
Totals		**168**	**3,901**	**2,025**	**51.9**	**27,989**	**7.17**	**212**	**210**	**70.9**	**444**	**2,257**	**32**

*Led league

Transactions
- Selected by Pittsburgh Steelers in the first round (first pick overall) of the 1970 NFL Draft;
- On injured reserve with elbow injury (August 30–December 2, 1983).

Noteworthy
- Inducted into Pro Football Hall of Fame in 1989;
- Selected to play in three Pro Bowls (following 1975, 1978, and 1979 seasons);
- 1978 NFL player of the year;
- Guided Steelers to victories in Super Bowls IX, X, XIII, and XIV;
- Completed 9 of 14 passes for 96 yards and 1 touchdown in IX;
- Completed 9 of 19 passes for 209 yards and 2 touchdowns in X;
- Completed 17 of 30 passes for 318 yards and 4 touchdowns and won MVP award in XIII;
- Completed 14 of 21 for 309 yards and 2 touchdowns and won MVP award in XIV;
- Super Bowl's all-time leader in: highest average gain, career (11.1) and game (14.7, XIV);
- Second in Super Bowl history for career touchdown passes (9);
- Third in Super Bowl history for: passer rating (112.8) and passing yards (932);
- Tied for third in Super Bowl history for touchdown passes in a game (4);
- Punted 5 times for 34.6-yard average (1980);
- Threw pass that was deflected and caught by Franco Harris for a 60-yard touchdown in the final seconds of a 1972 AFC Divisional Playoff, known as the "Immaculate Reception";
- Pittsburgh had never won a postseason game in its 37-year history when they drafted Bradshaw with the first overall pick in 1970; 10 years later, the Steelers had four Super Bowl rings;
- Has served as FOX studio host since 1994.

TOM BRADY (for more information, see pages 94–95)

| YEAR | TEAM | G | ATT | COMP | PCT | YDS | YPA | TD | INT | RATING | RUSHING | | |
											ATT	YDS	TD
2000	New England	1	3	1	33.3	6	2.00	0	0	42.4	0	0	0
2001	New England	15	413	264	63.9	2,843	6.88	18	12	86.5	36	43	
2002	New England	16	601	373	62.1	3,764	6.26	28*	14	85.7	42	110	
Totals		**32**	**1,017**	**638**	**62.7**	**6,613**	**6.50**	**46**	**26**	**85.9**	**78**	**153**	

*Led league

Transactions
- Selected by New England Patriots in the sixth round (199th pick overall) of the 2000 NFL Draft.

Noteworthy
- Selected to one Pro Bowl (following the 2001 season);
- Brady is one of six quarterbacks since 1970 to be selected to the Pro Bowl in his first year as a starter (Dan Marino, Bratt Favre, Kurt Warner, Daunte Culpepper, and Michael Vick are the others);
- Starting quarterback for Patriots' Super Bowl XXXVI victory;
- Completed 16 of 27 passes for 145 yards and 1 touchdown and won MVP award for New England's Super Bowl XXXVI triumph;
- Brady was the second quarterback to win the Super Bowl in the year of his first career start (Kurt Warner, St. Louis, Super Bowl XXXIV is the other);
- Replaced injured Drew Bledsoe in fourth quarter of second game of 2001 season;
- Guided Patriots to 11–3 record the remainder of the 2001 season;
- In his first postseason game, set club records for passing yards (312) and completions (32) in the 2001 AFC Divisional Playoff victory against Oakland;
- Prior to Brady's arrival, the Patriots' club record for completion percentage was 61.6. Tom broke that figure in each of his first two seasons;
- In 2002, became first Patriots quarterback to lead the NFL in touchdown passes for a season (in 1979, Patriots' Steve Grogan had tied for the NFL lead in touchdown passes);
- In 2000, spent 14 weeks as the third quarterback;
- Only playing time in 2000 came in the fourth quarter of a Thanksgiving Day blowout defeat at Detroit;
- Drafted as a catcher by the Montreal Expos in the eighteenth round of the 1995 baseball draft;
- During his sophomore year, Brady served as Brian Griese's backup as the University of Michigan won the 1997 national championship.
- At 24 years, 184 days old, was the youngest quarterback to win a Super Bowl.

AARON BROOKS (for more information, see pages 26–27)

YEAR	TEAM	G	ATT	COMP	PCT	YDS	YPA	TD	INT	RATING	RUSHING ATT	RUSHING YDS	RUSHING TD
1999	Green Bay				*DID NOT PLAY*								
2000	New Orleans	8	194	113	58.2	1,514	7.80	9	6	85.7	41	170	2
2001	New Orleans	16	558	312	55.9	3,832	6.87	26	22	76.4	80	358	1
2002	New Orleans	16	528	283	53.6	3,572	6.77	27	15	80.1	61	256	2
Totals		40	1,280	708	55.3	8,918	6.97	64	62	79.4	182	784	5

Transactions
- Selected by Green Bay Packers in fourth round (131st pick overall) of the 1999 NFL Draft;
- Traded by Packers with TE Lamont Hall to New Orleans Saints for LB K.D. Williams and third-round pick (traded to San Francisco) in 2001 NFL Draft (July 31, 2000).

Noteworthy
- Guided Saints to first postseason victory, with 4 touchdown passes in 2000 NFC Wild Card Game against the defending-champion St. Louis Rams;
- In two postseason games, has a 92.0 passer rating and 6 touchdown passes;
- First player in NFL history to post a 400-yard passing game and 100-yard rushing game in the same season (441 passing yards vs. Denver, Dec. 3, 2000, and 108 rushing yards at San Francisco, December 10, 2000)
- Set club record for touchdown passes in a season (27) in 2002 after tying record (26) in 2001;
- Set club record for passing yards in a game (441 vs. Denver, Dec. 3, 2000);
- Set club record for rushing yards in a game by quarterback (108 at San Francisco, Dec. 10, 2000) and in a season (358 in 2001);
- Set club record for total yards in a season (4,190 in 2001). In two seasons as a full-time starter, owns the first- and fourth-best total yardage seasons in club history;
- In 2002, tied for first in NFC in touchdown passes (27);
- Listed as Green Bay's third quarterback in 1999, behind Brett Favre and Matt Hasselbeck;
- Saints traded for Brooks at the behest of offensive coordinator Mike McCarthy, who joined the Saints in 2000 after serving as the Packers' quarterbacks coach in 1999;
- Is the second cousin of Atlanta Falcons quarterback Michael Vick.

MARK BRUNELL (for more information, see pages 28–29)

YEAR	TEAM	G	ATT	COMP	PCT	YDS	YPA	TD	INT	RATING	RUSHING ATT	YDS	TD
1993	Green Bay					DID NOT PLAY							
1994	Green Bay	2	27	12	44.4	95	3.52	0	0	53.8	6	7	1
1995	Jacksonville	13	346	201	58.1	2,168	6.27	15	7	82.6	67	480	4
1996	Jacksonville	16	557	353	63.4	4,367*	7.84*	19	20	84.0	80	396	3
1997	Jacksonville	14	435	264	60.7	3,281	7.54	18	7	91.2	48	257	2
1998	Jacksonville	13	354	208	58.8	2,601	7.35	20	9	89.9	49	192	0
1999	Jacksonville	15	441	259	58.7	3,060	6.94	14	9	82.0	47	208	1
2000	Jacksonville	16	512	311	60.7	3,640	7.11	20	14	84.0	48	236	2
2001	Jacksonville	15	473	289	61.1	3,309	7.00	19	13	84.1	39	224	1
2002	Jacksonville	15	416	245	58.9	2,788	6.70	17	7	85.7	43	207	0
Totals		**119**	**3,561**	**2,142**	**60.2**	**25,309**	**7.11**	**142**	**86**	**85.1**	**427**	**2,207**	**14**

*Led league

Transactions
- Selected by Green Bay Packers in the fifth round (118th pick overall) of the 1993 NFL Draft;
- Traded by Packers to Jacksonville Jaguars for third- (FB William Henderson) and fifth-round (RB Travis Jervey) picks in 1995 NFL Draft (April 21, 1995).

Noteworthy
- Selected to Pro Bowl (following the 1996, 1997, and 1999 seasons);
- Jaguars' leading passer all eight years in franchise history;
- Entered 2003 as seventh-best passer (85.1) in NFL history;
- Only quarterback ranked among the top 11 passers each season from 1996–2002;
- Jaguars are 63–51 when he starts, 5–9 when he is injured and doesn't start;
- Brunell is particularly tough in divisional games, posting a 37–21 (.638) record;
- Of Brunell's 142 touchdown passes, Jimmy Smith has been his number-one target (44 touchdown catches), Keenan McCardell is second (26), and Damon Jones is third (11);
- Became starter in sixth game of 1995 season, replacing Steve Beuerlein;
- Mark's 4 rushing touchdowns in 1995 led the club;
- In just the franchise's second season, passed for 239 yards as Jacksonville defeated Buffalo in a 1996 AFC Wild Card Game, and passed for 245 yards and 2 touchdowns as the Jaguars shocked the number-one seeded Broncos in an AFC Divisional Playoff Game;
- Passed for a career high 432 yards at New England in 1996;
- A four-time all-league baseball selection in high school, Mark was drafted by the Atlanta Braves in the 44th round of the 1992 draft;
- 2002 NFLPA's Byron (Whizzer) White Humanitarian Award winner for his commitment to community causes.

DAUNTE CULPEPPER (for more information, see pages 30–31)

YEAR	TEAM	G	ATT	COMP	PCT	YDS	YPA	TD	INT	RATING	RUSHING ATT	RUSHING YDS	RUSHING TD
1999	Minnesota	1	0	0	—	0	—	0	0	—	3	6	0
2000	Minnesota	16	474	297	62.7	3,937	8.31	33	16	98.0	89	470	7
2001	Minnesota	11	366	235	64.2	2,612	7.14	14	13	83.3	71	416	5
2002	Minnesota	16	549	333	60.7	3,853	7.02	18	23*	75.3	106	609	10
Totals		**44**	**1,389**	**865**	**62.3**	**10,402**	**7.49**	**65**	**52**	**85.2**	**269**	**1,501**	**22**

Transactions
• Selected by Minnesota Vikings in the first round (11th pick overall) of the 1999 NFL Draft.

Noteworthy
• Selected to Pro Bowl (following the 2000 season);
• A true double threat, Culpepper has both run and passed for a touchdown in 15 of his 43 career starts (4 times in 2000, 4 times in 2001, and 7 times in 2002);
• Set NFL mark for most rushing touchdowns (22) by a quarterback in first four seasons, breaking record set by New England's Steve Grogan (21 from 1975–78);
• Just the third quarterback in NFL history to rush for 5 touchdowns in three consecutive seasons (Cleveland's Otto Graham, 1953–55, and Green Bay's Tobin Rote, 1954–56);
• Culpepper and running back Moe Williams each rushed for at least 10 touchdowns in 2002, becoming the third pair of teammates to rush for 10 touchdowns in a season [Green Bay, 1960, Paul Hornung (13) and Jim Taylor (11); and Baltimore Colts, 1975, Lydell Mitchell (11), and Don McCauley (10)];
• Set club single-season record with 470 rushing yards in 2000 (breaking Fran Tarkenton's record of 376 in 1966), and then broke his own record in 2002 with 609 rushing yards;
• Set club single-season record with 7 rushing touchdowns by a quarterback in 2000 (breaking the record of 5 held by Fran Tarkenton, 1961, and Wade Wilson, 1987), and then broke his own record in 2002 with 10 rushing touchdowns;
• Tied for first in club history, with Fran Tarkenton, for rushing touchdowns by a quarterback (22);
• Became the first quarterback in Vikings history to win his first 7 starts;
• First in club history by completing at least 60 percent of his passes in 23 starts;
• Set club single-season record with seven games with at least 3 passing touchdowns (2000);
• Joined Tommy Kramer and Warren Moon as only Vikings with multiple 3,000-yard seasons;
• Tied for second in club single-season history with 33 touchdown passes (2000);
• Ranks third and fifth in club single-season history with 3,937 and 3,853 passing yards (2000 and 2002);
• Set NCAA record his senior season at Central Florida by completing 73.6 percent of his passes, breaking 15-year-old record held by Brigham Young's Steve Young;
• Was born to a mother who was serving time in prison and was adopted by a prison worker, who raised him in Ocala, Florida.

RANDALL CUNNINGHAM (for more information, see pages 72–73)

YEAR	TEAM	G	ATT	COMP	PCT	YDS	YPA	TD	INT	RATING	RUSHING ATT	YDS	TD
1985	Philadelphia	6	81	34	42.0	548	6.77	1	8	29.8	29	205	0
1986	Philadelphia	15	209	111	53.1	1,391	6.66	8	7	72.9	66	540	5
1987	Philadelphia	12	406	223	54.9	2,786	6.86	23	12	83.0	76	505	3
1988	Philadelphia	16	560	301	53.8	3,808	6.80	24	16	77.6	93	624	6
1989	Philadelphia	16	532	290	54.5	3,400	6.39	21	15	75.5	104	621	4
1990	Philadelphia	16	465	271	58.3	3,466	7.45	30	13	91.6	118	942	5
1991	Philadelphia	1	4	1	25.0	19	4.75	0	0	46.9	0	0	0
1992	Philadelphia	15	384	233	60.7	2,775	7.23	19	11	87.3	87	549	5
1993	Philadelphia	4	110	76	69.1	850	7.73	5	5	88.1	18	110	1
1994	Philadelphia	14	490	265	54.1	3,229	6.59	16	13	74.4	65	288	3
1995	Philadelphia	7	121	69	57.0	605	5.00	3	5	61.5	21	98	0
1996						OUT OF FOOTBALL							
1997	Minnesota	6	88	44	50.0	501	5.69	6	4	71.3	19	127	0
1998	Minnesota	15	425	259	60.9	3,704	8.72	34	10	106.0*	32	132	1
1999	Minnesota	6	200	124	62.0	1,475	7.38	8	9	79.1	10	58	0
2000	Dallas	6	125	74	59.2	849	6.79	6	4	82.4	23	89	1
2001	Baltimore	6	89	54	60.7	573	6.44	3	2	81.3	14	40	1
Totals		**161**	**4,289**	**2,429**	**56.6**	**29,979**	**6.99**	**207**	**134**	**81.5**	**775**	**4,928**	**35**

*Led league

Transactions
- Selected by Arizona Outlaws in 1985 USFL territorial draft, but never played in USFL;
- Selected by Philadelphia Eagles in the second round (37th pick overall) of the 1985 NFL Draft;
- On injured reserve with knee injury (Sept. 3–end of 1991 season);
- On retired list (Aug. 30, 1996–April 15, 1997), signed with Minnesota Vikings (April 15, 1997);
- Released by Vikings (June 2, 2000), signed with Dallas Cowboys (June 8, 2000);
- Granted unconditional free agency, signed with Baltimore Ravens (May 29, 2001).

Noteworthy
- Selected to four Pro Bowls (following the 1988–1990 and 1998 seasons);
- Holds NFL mark for rushing yards by a quarterback (4,928);
- Quarterback of 1998 Vikings, who scored an NFL record 556 points;
- Set Eagles single-season record for passing yards (3,808 in 1988);
- Set Eagles single-game record for passing yards (447 at Washington, Sept. 17, 1989);
- Also punted 12 times for 620 yards (51.7 average) and had 2 receptions in his career;
- Has the longest punt (91 yards) and tied for third-longest punt (80 yards) in Eagles history;
- Cunningham averaged 45.6 yards per punt during his collegiate career, and was selected as an all-conference quarterback and punter his junior and senior seasons at UNLV;
- His brother, Sam, was a running back for the New England Patriots (1973–1979, 1981–82).

LEN DAWSON (for more information, see pages 74–75)

YEAR	TEAM	G	ATT	COMP	PCT	YDS	YPA	TD	INT	RATING	RUSHING ATT	YDS	TD
1957	Pittsburgh	3	4	2	50.0	25	6.25	0	0	69.8	3	31	0
1958	Pittsburgh	4	6	1	16.7	11	1.83	0	2	0.0	2	-1	0
1959	Pittsburgh	12	7	3	42.9	60	8.57	1	0	113.1	4	20	0
1960	Cleveland	2	13	8	61.5	23	1.77	0	0	65.9	1	0	0
1961	Cleveland	7	15	7	46.7	85	5.67	1	3	47.2	1	-10	0
1962	Dallas Texans	14	310	189	61.0*	2,759	8.90*	29*	17	98.3	38	252	3
1963	Kansas City	14	352	190	54.0	2,389	6.79	26	19	77.5	37	272	2
1964	Kansas City	14	354	199	56.2*	2,879	8.13	30	18	89.9	40	89	2
1965	Kansas City	14	305	163	53.4*	2,262	7.42	21*	14	81.3	43	142	2
1966	Kansas City	14	284	159	56.0*	2,527	8.90*	26*	10	101.7	24	167	0
1967	Kansas City	14	357	206	57.7*	2,651	7.43	24	17	83.7	20	68	0
1968	Kansas City	14	224	131	58.5*	2,109	9.42*	17	9	98.6	20	40	0
1969	Kansas City	9	166	98	59.0*	1,323	7.97	9	13	69.9	1	3	0
1970	Kansas City	14	262	141	53.8	1,876	7.16	13	14	71.0	11	46	0
1971	Kansas City	14	301	167	55.5	2,504	8.32	15	13	81.6	12	24	0
1972	Kansas City	14	305	175	57.4	1,835	6.02	13	12	72.8	15	75	0
1973	Kansas City	8	101	66	65.3	725	7.18	2	5	72.4	6	40	0
1974	Kansas City	14	235	138	58.7	1,573	6.69	7	13	65.8	11	28	0
1975	Kansas City	12	140	93	66.4*	1,095	7.82	5	4	90.0	5	7	0
Totals		211	3,741	2,136	57.1	28,711	7.67	239	183	82.6	294	1,293	9

*Led league

Transactions

- Selected by Pittsburgh Steelers in the first round (fifth pick overall) of the 1957 NFL Draft;
- Traded with WR Gern Nagler by Steelers to Cleveland Browns for WR Preston Carpenter and CB Lowe Wren (Jan. 13, 1960);
- Released by Browns, signed by Dallas Texans of the AFL (1962);
- Texans relocated and named Kansas City Chiefs (1963).

Noteworthy

- Inducted into Pro Football Hall of Fame in 1987;
- Selected to seven AFL All-Star Games/Pro Bowls (after 1962, 1964, 1966–69, and 1971 seasons);
- Guided Texans/Chiefs to AFL championships in 1962, 1966, and 1969, and Super Bowl IV title;
- Passed for 1 touchdown as Texans won 1962 AFL Championship Game in double overtime;
- Completed 16 of 27 passes for 211 yards and 1 touchdown in Super Bowl I;
- Completed 12 of 17 passes for 142 yards and 1 touchdown and was named MVP in Kansas City's Super Bowl IV victory;
- His uniform number 16 was retired by the Chiefs;
- Chiefs' record holder for passer rating (83.2), passing yards (28,507), completions (2,115), and touchdown passes (237);
- Served as commentator on HBO's *Inside the NFL* for nearly a quarter century.

JOHN ELWAY (for more information, see pages 12–13)

Year	Team	G	Att	Comp	Pct	Yds	YPA	TD	Int	Rating	Rushing Att	Yds	TD
1983	Denver	11	259	123	47.5	1,663	6.42	7	14	54.9	28	146	
1984	Denver	15	380	215	56.3	2,598	6.84	18	15	76.8	56	237	
1985	Denver	16	605*	327	54.0	3,891	6.43	22	23	70.2	51	253	
1986	Denver	16	504	280	55.6	3,485	6.91	19	13	79.0	52	257	
1987	Denver	12	410	224	54.6	3,198	7.80	19	12	83.4	66	304	
1988	Denver	15	496	274	55.2	3,309	6.67	17	19	71.4	54	234	
1989	Denver	15	416	223	53.6	3,051	7.33	18	18	73.7	48	244	
1990	Denver	16	502	294	58.6	3,526	7.02	15	14	78.5	50	258	
1991	Denver	16	451	242	53.7	3,253	7.21	13	12	75.4	55	255	
1992	Denver	12	316	174	55.1	2,242	7.09	10	17	65.7	34	94	
1993	Denver	16	551*	348*	63.2	4,030*	7.31	24	10	92.8	44	153	
1994	Denver	14	494	307	62.1	3,490	7.06	16	10	85.7	58	235	
1995	Denver	16	542	316	58.3	3,970	7.32	26	14	86.4	41	176	
1996	Denver	15	466	287	61.6	3,328	7.14	26	14	89.2	50	249	
1997	Denver	16	502	280	55.8	3,635	7.24	27	11	87.5	50	218	
1998	Denver	13	356	210	59.0	2,806	7.88	22	10	93.0	37	94	
Totals		**234**	**7,250**	**4,123**	**56.9**	**51,475**	**7.10**	**300**	**226**	**79.9**	**774**	**3,407**	**3**

*Led league

Transactions
- Selected by Oakland Invaders in 1983 USFL territorial draft, but never played in USFL;
- Selected by Baltimore Colts in the first round (first pick overall) of the 1983 NFL Draft;
- Traded by Colts to Denver Broncos for QB Mark Herrmann, T Chris Hinton, and 1984 first-round pick (G Ron Solt) (May 2, 1983).

Noteworthy
- Selected to nine Pro Bowls (following the 1986, 1987, 1989, 1991, 1993, 1994, and 1996–98 seasons);
- 1987 NFL most valuable player;
- Guided Broncos to five Super Bowls, the most by a quarterback in NFL history;
- Completed 22 of 37 passes for 304 yards and 1 touchdown in XXI;
- Completed 14 of 38 passes for 257 yards and 1 touchdown in XXII;
- Completed 10 of 26 passes for 108 yards in XXIV;
- Completed 12 of 22 passes for 123 yards and ran for 1 touchdown in Broncos' victory in XXXII;
- Completed 18 of 29 passes for 336 yards and 1 touchdown, ran for a score, and was named MVP of Broncos' XXXIII victory;
- His uniform number 7 was retired by the Broncos (1999);
- Owns record for most career victories by a quarterback (148);
- NFL leader in career rushing attempts by a quarterback, and fourth in rushing yards;
- Only quarterback to pass for 3,000 yards and run for 200 yards in seven consecutive seasons;
- Guided Broncos to 33 come-from-behind fourth-quarter comebacks (including postseason).

BOOMER ESIASON

(for more information, see pages 96–97)

Year	Team	G	Att	Comp	Pct	Yds	YPA	TD	Int	Rating	Att	Yds	TD
											Rushing		
1984	Cincinnati	10	102	51	50.0	530	5.20	3	3	62.9	19	63	2
1985	Cincinnati	15	431	251	58.2	3,443	7.99	27	12	93.2	33	79	1
1986	Cincinnati	16	469	273	58.2	3,959	8.44*	24	17	87.7	44	146	1
1987	Cincinnati	12	440	240	54.5	3,321	7.55	16	19	73.1	52	241	0
1988	Cincinnati	16	388	223	57.5	3,572	9.21*	28	14	97.4*	43	248	1
1989	Cincinnati	16	455	258	56.7	3,525	7.75	28	11	92.1	47	278	0
1990	Cincinnati	16	402	224	55.7	3,031	7.54	24	22	77.0	49	157	0
1991	Cincinnati	14	413	233	56.4	2,883	6.98	13	16	72.5	24	66	0
1992	Cincinnati	12	278	144	51.8	1,407	5.06	11	15	57.0	21	66	0
1993	N.Y. Jets	16	473	288	60.9	3,421	7.23	16	11	84.5	45	118	0
1994	N.Y. Jets	15	440	255	58.0	2,782	6.32	17	13	77.3	28	59	0
1995	N.Y. Jets	12	389	221	56.8	2,275	5.85	16	15	71.4	19	14	0
1996	Arizona	10	339	190	56.0	2,293	6.76	11	14	70.6	15	52	1
1997	Cincinnati	7	186	118	63.4	1,478	7.95	13	2	106.9	8	11	0
Totals		**187**	**5,205**	**2,969**	**57.0**	**37,920**	**7.29**	**247**	**184**	**81.1**	**447**	**1,598**	**7**

*Led league

Transactions

- Selected by Washington Federals in 1984 USFL territorial draft, but never played in USFL;
- Selected by Cincinnati Bengals in second round (38th pick overall) of the 1984 NFL Draft;
- Traded by Bengals to N.Y. Jets for third-round pick (DT Ty Parten) in 1993 NFL Draft (March 17, 1993);
- Granted unconditional free agency, signed with Arizona Cardinals (April 8, 1996);
- Released by Cardinals, signed with Cincinnati Bengals (April 5, 1997).

Noteworthy

- Selected to four Pro Bowls (following the 1986, 1988, 1989, and 1993 seasons);
- Guided Bengals to AFC title and appearance in Super Bowl XXIII;
- Completed 11 of 25 passes for 144 yards in XXIII;
- Third in NFL history in passing yards in a game (522 yards at Washington, Nov. 10, 1996);
- Also punted 4 times for 120 yards (30.0 average) and caught 1 pass;
- First in Bengals history in passing yards in a season (3,959 in 1986);
- First in Bengals history in passing yards in a game (490 at L.A. Rams, Oct. 7, 1990);
- Is the only Bengals quarterback to pass for 5 touchdowns in a game, and did it twice (vs. N.Y. Jets, Dec. 21, 1986, and vs. Tampa Bay, Oct. 29, 1989);
- First in Bengals history in career passer rating (83.1) and in yards per attempt (7.62);
- Served two seasons as commentator on ABC's *NFL Monday Night Football*, has been a studio analyst on CBS, and color commentator on CBS/Westwood One radio;
- Real first name is Norman. Nicknamed "Boomer" because he kicked so much during his mother's pregnancy.

BRETT FAVRE (for more information, see pages 52–53)

YEAR	TEAM	G	ATT	COMP	PCT	YDS	YPA	TD	INT	RATING	RUSHING ATT	RUSHING YDS	RUSHING TD
1991	Atlanta	2	5	0	0.0	0	0.00	0	2	0.0	0	0	0
1992	Green Bay	15	471	302	64.1	3,227	6.85	18	13	85.3	47	198	1
1993	Green Bay	16	522	318	60.9	3,303	6.33	19	24*	72.2	58	216	1
1994	Green Bay	16	582	363	62.4	3,882	6.67	33	14	90.7	42	202	2
1995	Green Bay	16	570	359	63.0	4,413*	7.74	38*	13	99.5	39	181	3
1996	Green Bay	16	543	325	59.9	3,899	7.18	39*	13	95.8	49	136	2
1997	Green Bay	16	513	304	59.3	3,867	7.54	35*	16	92.6	58	187	1
1998	Green Bay	16	551	347*	63.0*	4,212*	7.64	31	23	87.8	40	133	1
1999	Green Bay	16	595*	341	57.3	4,091	6.88	22	23	74.7	28	142	0
2000	Green Bay	16	580	338	58.3	3,812	6.57	20	16	78.0	27	108	0
2001	Green Bay	16	510	315	61.6	3,921	7.69	32	15	94.1	38	56	1
2002	Green Bay	16	551	341	61.9	3,658	6.64	27	16	85.6	25	73	0
Totals		**177**	**5,993**	**3,652**	**60.9**	**42,285**	**7.06**	**314**	**188**	**86.7**	**451**	**1,632**	**12**

*Led league

Transactions
- Selected by Atlanta Falcons in the second round (33rd pick overall) of the 1991 NFL Draft;
- Traded by Falcons to Green Bay Packers for first-round pick (T Bob Whitfield) in 1992 NFL Draft (Feb. 11, 1992).

Noteworthy
- Selected to seven Pro Bowls (following the 1992, 1993, 1995–97, 2001, and 2002 seasons);
- NFL's only three-time most valuable player (1995, 1996, and 1997);
- Guided the Packers to Super Bowls XXXI and XXXII;
- Completed 14 of 27 passes for 246 yards and 2 touchdowns in Packers' XXXI victory;
- Completed 25 of 42 passes for 256 yards and 3 touchdowns in XXXII;
- Entered 2003 with 173 consecutive starts, the longest streak ever by an NFL quarterback;
- Has passed for at least 30 touchdowns an NFL record six times;
- First NFL quarterback to post 11 consecutive 3,000-yard seasons;
- Owns NFL quarterback record by posting 11 consecutive seasons with at least 8 victories;
- Owns best home winning percentage (.867, 78–12) by quarterback whose career began after 196
- Third in NFL history with 314 touchdown passes;
- Tied for first in postseason history with a touchdown pass in 13 consecutive games;
- 99-yard touchdown pass to Robert Brooks equals the longest in NFL history (vs. Chicago, Sept. 11, 1995);
- Favre is 35–1 (including postseason) in home games with the temperature 34 degrees or below;
- N.Y. Jets director of player personnel Ron Wolf was going to select Favre with the 34th pick of the 1991 NFL Draft, but Atlanta selected him with the pick prior to the Jets' choice; Wolf then became the Packers general manager and traded for Favre in February 1992.

DAN FOUTS (for more information, see pages 98–99)

YEAR	TEAM	G	ATT	COMP	PCT	YDS	YPA	TD	INT	RATING	RUSHING ATT	RUSHING YDS	RUSHING TD
1973	San Diego	10	194	87	44.8	1,126	5.80	6	13	46.0	7	32	0
1974	San Diego	11	237	115	48.5	1,732	7.31	8	13	61.4	19	63	1
1975	San Diego	10	195	106	54.4	1,396	7.16	2	10	59.3	23	170	2
1976	San Diego	14	359	208	57.9	2,535	7.06	14	15	75.4	18	65	0
1977	San Diego	4	109	69	63.3	869	7.97	4	6	77.4	6	13	0
1978	San Diego	15	381	224	58.8	2,999	7.87	24	20	83.0	20	43	2
1979	San Diego	16	530	332	62.6*	4,082*	7.70	24	24	82.6	26	49	2
1980	San Diego	16	589*	348*	59.1	4,715*	8.01	30	24	84.7	23	15	2
1981	San Diego	16	609*	360*	59.1	4,802*	7.89	33*	17	90.6	22	56	0
1982	San Diego	9	330	204	61.8	2,883*	8.74*	17*	11	93.3	9	8	1
1983	San Diego	10	340	215	63.2	2,975	8.75	20	15	92.5	12	-5	1
1984	San Diego	13	507	317	62.5	3,740	7.38	19	17	83.4	12	-29	0
1985	San Diego	14	430	254	59.1	3,638	8.46*	27	20	88.1	11	-1	0
1986	San Diego	12	430	252	58.6	3,031	7.05	16	22	71.4	4	-3	0
1987	San Diego	11	364	206	56.6	2,517	6.91	10	15	70.0	12	0	2
Totals		**181**	**5,604**	**3,297**	**58.8**	**43,040**	**7.68**	**254**	**242**	**80.2**	**224**	**476**	**13**

Led league

Transactions
- Selected by San Diego Chargers in the third round (64th pick overall) of the 1973 NFL Draft;
- On injured reserve list with knee injury (Dec. 8–end of 1984 season).

Noteworthy
- Selected to six Pro Bowls (following the 1979–1983 and 1985 seasons);
- His uniform number 14 is the only jersey retired by the Chargers;
- Averaged 320.3 passing yards per game in 1982, highest ever;
- Passed for at least 300 yards in a record 4 consecutive postseason games;
- Tied for most consecutive 400-yard games in NFL history (2 in 1982);
- Second in NFL history for 300-yard passing games (51);
- Passed for 4,802 yards in 1981, third-highest single-season total in NFL history;
- Tied for third-most seasons leading the NFL in passing yards (4 times, 1979–1982);
- Fourth in NFL history for 400-yard passing games (6);
- Set the NFL single-season passing yardage record in 1979, and then broke his own record each of the next two seasons;
- Owns every club single-game, single-season, and career passing record;
- As a rookie in 1973, replaced an aging and injured Johnny Unitas in the starting lineup;
- Spent two seasons on ABC's *NFL Monday Night Football* broadcast crew (2000 and 2001);
- Wide receiver and Fouts' teammate Wes Chandler: "When you have a pure passer such as Dan, from a receiver's standpoint, it's like dying and going to heaven."

RICH GANNON (for more information, see pages 32–33)

YEAR	TEAM	G	ATT	COMP	PCT	YDS	YPA	TD	INT	RATING	ATT	YDS	TD
1987	Minnesota	4	6	2	33.3	18	3.00	0	1	2.8	0	0	0
1988	Minnesota	3	15	7	46.7	90	6.00	0	0	66.0	4	29	0
1989	Minnesota				DID NOT PLAY								
1990	Minnesota	14	349	182	52.1	2,278	6.53	16	16	68.9	52	268	
1991	Minnesota	15	354	211	59.6	2,166	6.12	12	6	81.5	43	236	
1992	Minnesota	12	279	159	57.0	1,905	6.83	12	13	72.9	45	187	
1993	Washington	8	125	74	59.2	704	5.63	3	7	59.6	21	88	
1994					OUT OF FOOTBALL								
1995	Kansas City	2	11	7	63.6	57	5.18	0	0	76.7	8	25	
1996	Kansas City	4	90	54	60.0	491	5.46	6	1	92.4	12	81	
1997	Kansas City	9	175	98	56.0	1,144	6.54	7	4	79.8	33	109	
1998	Kansas City	12	354	206	58.2	2,305	6.51	10	6	80.1	44	168	
1999	Oakland	16	515	304	59.0	3,840	7.46	24	14	86.5	46	298	
2000	Oakland	16	473	284	60.0	3,430	7.25	28	11	92.4	89	529	
2001	Oakland	16	549	361	65.8	3,828	6.97	27	9	95.5	63	231	
2002	Oakland	16	618*	418*	67.6	4,689*	7.59	26	10	97.3	50	156	
Totals		**147**	**3,913**	**2,367**	**60.5**	**26,945**	**6.89**	**171**	**98**	**85.3**	**510**	**2,405**	**2**

*Led league

Transactions
- Selected by New England Patriots in the fourth round (98th pick overall) of the 1987 NFL Draft
- Traded by Patriots to Minnesota Vikings for fourth- (WR Sammy Martin) and eleventh-round (traded) picks in 1988 NFL Draft (May 6, 1987);
- Traded by Vikings to Washington Redskins for fifth-round pick (CB Shelly Hammonds) in the 1994 NFL Draft (Aug. 20, 1993);
- Granted unconditional free agency, signed by Kansas City Chiefs (March 29, 1995);
- Granted unconditional free agency, signed by Oakland Raiders (Feb. 16, 1999).

Noteworthy
- Selected to four Pro Bowls (following the 1999–2002 seasons);
- 2002 NFL most valuable player;
- 2001 and 2002 Pro Bowl player of the game…first player to win the award in consecutive game
- Guided the Raiders to AFC title and berth in Super Bowl XXXVII;
- Completed 24 of 44 passes for 272 yards and 2 touchdowns in XXXVII;
- Set NFL record for completions in a season (418 in 2002);
- Completed 21 consecutive passes to set NFL single-game record (vs. Denver, Nov. 11, 2002);
- Established NFL record for most 300-yard passing games in a season (10 in 2002);
- Second in NFL history with 43 completions in a game (at Pittsburgh, Sept. 15, 2002);
- First in Raiders history in completion percentage (63.4).

JEFF GARCIA (for more information, see pages 34–35)

YEAR	TEAM	G	ATT	COMP	PCT	YDS	YPA	TD	INT	RATING	RUSHING ATT	RUSHING YDS	RUSHING TD
1994	Calgary (CFL)	7	3	2	66.7	10	3.33	0	0	—	2	3	0
1995	Calgary (CFL)	18	364	230	63.2	3,358	9.23	25	7	—	61	396	5
1996	Calgary (CFL)	18	537	315	58.7	4,225	7.87	25	16	—	92	657	6
1997	Calgary (CFL)	17	566	354	62.5	4,568	8.07	33	14	—	134	739	7
1998	Calgary (CFL)	18	554	348	62.8	4,276	7.72	28	15	—	94	575	6
1999	San Francisco	13	375	225	60.0	2,544	6.78	11	11	77.9	45	231	2
2000	San Francisco	16	561	355	63.3	4,278	7.63	31	10	97.6	72	414	4
2001	San Francisco	16	504	316	62.7	3,538	7.02	32	12	94.8	72	254	5
2002	San Francisco	16	528	328	62.1	3,344	6.33	21	10	85.6	73	353	3
CFL Totals		**78**	**2,024**	**1,249**	**61.7**	**16,437**	**8.12**	**111**	**52**	**—**	**383**	**2,370**	**24**
NFL Totals		**61**	**1,968**	**1,224**	**62.2**	**13,704**	**6.96**	**95**	**43**	**89.9**	**262**	**1,252**	**14**
Totals		**139**	**3,992**	**2,473**	**61.9**	**30,141**	**7.55**	**206**	**95**	**—**	**645**	**3,622**	**38**

ˈLed league

Transactions

- Signed by the Calgary Stampeders (CFL) in 1994;
- Signed by San Francisco 49ers as a nondrafted free agent (Feb. 16, 1999).

Noteworthy

- Selected to three Pro Bowls (following the 2000–2002 seasons);
- Owns best career touchdown-to-interception ratio in NFL history (95 to 43, 2.21 ratio);
- Fourth in NFL history for career passer rating (89.9), trailing only Kurt Warner, Steve Young, and Joe Montana;
- First player in 49ers history with consecutive 30-touchdown seasons (2000 and 2001);
- First player in 49ers history with three consecutive 300-completion seasons (2000–02);
- Joined Joe Montana and Steve Young as the only 49ers to pass for 3,000 yards three consecutive seasons (2000–02);
- First in club single-season history in passing yards (4,278 in 2000);
- First in club single-season history in completions (355 in 2000);
- Second in club single-game history in completions (36 vs. Chicago, Dec. 17, 2000);
- Second in club single-season history in 300-yard games (6 in 2000);
- Joined Warren Moon as only former Canadian Football League (CFL) quarterbacks with consecutive NFL seasons of 3,500 passing yards (2000 and 2001);
- Garcia uses his mobility as well as any quarterback—in 2002, he completed 65 of 89 passes (73 percent) while on the move, and averaged 6.9 yards per scramble;
- From 2000–02, Garcia rushed for 68 first downs;
- He also comes through in the clutch—in 2002, Garcia was the NFL's top-rated passer on third downs, posting a 107.6 passer rating;
- Jeff's father was the head coach his freshman year at Gavilan College, before Jeff transferred to San Jose State for his final three collegiate seasons.

OTTO GRAHAM (for more information, see pages 76–77)

YEAR	TEAM	G	ATT	COMP	PCT	YDS	YPA	TD	INT	RATING	RUSHING ATT	YDS	TD
1946	Cle. (AAFC)	14	174	95	54.6	1,834	10.54*	17*	5	112.1*	30	-125	1
1947	Cle. (AAFC)	14	269	163	60.6*	2,753*	10.23*	25*	11	109.2*	19	72	1
1948	Cle. (AAFC)	14	333	173	52.0	2,713*	8.15	25	15	85.6*	23	146	6
1949	Cle. (AAFC)	12	285	161*	56.5	2,785*	9.77*	19	10	97.5*	27	107	3
1950	Cleveland	12	253	137	54.2	1,943	7.68	14	20	64.7	55	145	6
1951	Cleveland	12	265	147	55.5	2,205	8.32	17	16	79.2	35	29	3
1952	Cleveland	12	364*	181*	49.7	2,816*	7.74	20*	24	66.6	42	130	4
1953	Cleveland	12	258	167	64.7*	2,722*	10.55*	11	9	99.7*	43	143	6
1954	Cleveland	12	240	142	59.2*	2,092	8.72	11	17	73.5	63	114	8
1955	Cleveland	12	185	98	53.0*	1,721	9.30*	15	8	94.0*	68	121	6
AAFC Totals		**54**	**1,061**	**592**	**55.8**	**10,085**	**9.51**	**86**	**41**	**99.1**	**99**	**200**	**11**
NFL Totals		**72**	**1,565**	**872**	**55.7**	**13,499**	**8.63***	**88**	**94**	**78.2**	**306**	**682**	**33**
Totals		**126**	**2,626**	**1,464**	**55.8**	**23,584**	**8.98**	**174**	**135**	**86.6**	**405**	**882**	**44**

*Led league

Transactions
- Selected by Detroit Lions in the first round (fourth overall pick) of the 1944 NFL Draft;
- Never contacted by Lions, signed with Cleveland Browns of the All-American Football Conference (AAFC) in 1946.

Noteworthy
- Inducted into Pro Football Hall of Fame in 1965;
- Selected AAFC player of the year (1947 and 1948);
- Selected NFL player of the year (1951, 1953, and 1955);
- Selected to five Pro Bowls (following the 1950–1954 seasons);
- Guided Browns to 10 title games in 10 seasons, winning seven times, including three NFL titles;
- Passed for 4 touchdowns for Browns in 1950 NFL Championship Game victory;
- Passed for 3 touchdowns and ran for 3 scores as Browns won 1954 NFL Championship Game;
- Passed for 2 touchdowns, and ran for 2 scores, as Browns won 1955 NFL Championship Game;
- His uniform number 14 was retired by the Browns;
- Originally retired after 1954 season, but during 1955 preseason was talked into returning for one final season by coach Paul Brown, which concluded with another NFL title;
- NFL career leader in average gain per pass attempt (8.63 yards);
- First in club single-season annals with 64.7 percent completion percentage (1953);
- Scored 33 rushing touchdowns on just 306 career NFL carries;
- Graham played two seasons for Paul Brown on the Great Lakes Naval Station team (1944 and 1945), and when Brown was hired as Cleveland's coach, he signed Graham to be his quarterback;
- A terrific athlete, Graham also played professional basketball as guard on the National Basketball League-champion Rochester Royals in 1946.

BOB GRIESE (for more information, see pages 14–15)

YEAR	TEAM	G	ATT	COMP	PCT	YDS	YPA	TD	INT	RATING	RUSHING ATT	YDS	TD
1967	Miami	12	331	166	50.2	2,005	6.06	15	18	61.6	37	157	1
1968	Miami	13	355	186	52.4	2,473	6.97	21	16	75.7	42	230	1
1969	Miami	9	252	121	48.0	1,695	6.73	10	16	56.9	21	102	0
1970	Miami	14	245	142	58.0	2,019	8.24	12	17	72.1	26	89	2
1971	Miami	14	263	145	55.1	2,089	7.94	19	9	90.9	26	82	0
1972	Miami	6	97	53	54.6	638	6.58	4	4	71.6	3	11	1
1973	Miami	13	218	116	53.2	1,422	6.52	17	8	84.3	13	20	0
1974	Miami	13	253	152	60.1	1,968	7.78	16	15	80.9	16	66	1
1975	Miami	10	191	118	61.8	1,693	8.86*	14	13	86.6	17	59	1
1976	Miami	13	272	162	59.6	2,097	7.71	11	12	78.9	23	108	0
1977	Miami	14	307	180	58.6	2,252	7.34	22*	13	87.8*	16	30	0
1978	Miami	11	235	148	63.0*	1,791	7.62	11	11	82.4	9	10	0
1979	Miami	14	310	176	56.8	2,160	6.97	14	16	72.0	11	30	0
1980	Miami	5	100	61	61.0	790	7.90	6	4	89.2	1	0	0
Totals		**161**	**3,429**	**1,926**	**56.2**	**25,092**	**7.32**	**192**	**172**	**77.1**	**261**	**994**	**7**

*Led league

Transactions
- Selected by the Dolphins in the first round (fourth overall pick) of the 1967 AFL-NFL Draft;
- On injured reserve with shoulder injury (Nov. 18–end of 1980 season).

Noteworthy
- Inducted into Pro Football Hall of Fame in 1990;
- Selected to eight AFL All-Star Games/Pro Bowls (following the 1967, 1968, 1970, 1971, 1973, 1977, and 1978 seasons);
- Guided Dolphins to Super Bowls VI, VII, and VIII;
- Completed 12 of 23 passes for 134 yards in VI;
- Completed 8 of 11 passes for 88 yards and 1 touchdown in Dolphins' victory in VII;
- Completed 6 of 7 passes for 73 yards in Dolphins' victory in VIII;
- His uniform number 12 was retired by the Dolphins (1982);
- Posted a .698 winning percentage (91–39–1) under head coach Don Shula (1970–1980);
- In 1972, suffered a broken right leg and dislocated ankle in the season's fifth game, but returned to help the Dolphins defeat Pittsburgh in the 1972 AFC Championship Game and then started Super Bowl VII as Dolphins completed the only undefeated, untied season in NFL history;
- Became fourteenth player to surpass 25,000 passing yards…but on the same day he reached the milestone, Griese suffered a shoulder injury that led to his retirement;
- Tried wearing contact lenses in 1977 preseason to correct amblyopia, but experienced double vision…he then switched to eyeglasses, which he wore for his final four seasons;
- Don Shula: "[Griese's] probably the most unselfish guy I've ever been around. He got as much of a thrill calling the right running play for a touchdown as he did connecting on a bomb."

JOHN HADL (for more information, see pages 100–101)

YEAR	TEAM	G	ATT	COMP	PCT	YDS	YPA	TD	INT	RATING	RUSHING		
											ATT	YDS	TD
1962	San Diego	14	260	107	41.2	1,632	6.28	15	24	43.3	40	139	1
1963	San Diego	14	64	28	43.8	502	7.84	6	6	63.4	8	26	0
1964	San Diego	14	274	147	53.6	2,157	7.87	18	15	78.7	20	70	1
1965	San Diego	14	348	174	50.0	2,798*	8.04*	20	21	71.3	28	91	1
1966	San Diego	14	375	200	53.3	2,846	7.59	23	14	83.0	38	95	2
1967	San Diego	14	427	217	50.8	3,365	7.88	24	22	74.5	37	107	3
1968	San Diego	14	440*	208*	47.3	3,473*	7.89	27*	32	64.5	23	14	2
1969	San Diego	14	324	158	48.8	2,253	6.95	10	11	67.8	26	109	2
1970	San Diego	14	327	162	49.5	2,388	7.30	22	15	77.1	28	188	1
1971	San Diego	14	431*	233*	54.1	3,075*	7.13	21*	25	68.9	18	75	1
1972	San Diego	14	370	190	51.4	2,449	6.62	15	26	56.7	22	99	1
1973	Los Angeles	14	258	135	52.3	2,008	7.78	22	11	88.8	14	5	0
1974	Los Angeles	6	115	53	46.1	680	5.91	5	6	57.9	11	28	0
1974	Green Bay	8	184	89	48.4	1,072	5.83	3	8	54.0	8	-3	0
1975	Green Bay	14	353	191	54.1	2,095	5.93	6	21	52.8	20	47	0
1976	Houston	14	113	60	53.1	634	5.61	7	8	60.9	7	11	0
1977	Houston	14	24	11	45.8	76	3.17	0	3	13.9	3	11	1
Totals		**224**	**4,687**	**2,363**	**50.4**	**33,503**	**7.15**	**244**	**268**	**67.4**	**351**	**1,112**	**16**

*Led league

Transactions
- Selected by San Diego Chargers in the third round (24th pick overall) of the 1962 AFL Draft;
- Traded by Chargers to Los Angeles Rams for DT Coy Bacon and RB Bob Thomas (Jan. 25, 1973);
- Traded by Rams to Green Bay Packers for first- (DT Mike Fanning), second- (CB Monte Jackson) and third-round (C Geoff Reece) draft choices in 1975 and first- (traded) and second-round (CB Pat Thomas) draft choices in 1976 (Oct. 22, 1974);
- Traded with CB Ken Ellis, a fourth-round (WR Steve Largent) draft pick in 1976, a third-round (RB Tim Wilson) draft choice in 1977, and cash by Packers to Houston Oilers for QB Lynn Dickey (April 2, 1976).

Noteworthy
- Selected to six Pro Bowls (following the 1964, 1965, 1968, 1969, 1972, and 1973 seasons);
- Only player to lead the AFL (1968) and NFL (1971) in touchdown passes;
- Tied for twelfth in career touchdown passes and ranks sixteenth in career passing yards;
- Was the Chargers' main punter in 1964 and 1965 (including a 40.6-yard average in 1965);
- When the Oilers traded for Hadl in 1976, one of the draft picks they received was used to select future Pro Football Hall of Fame wide receiver Steve Largent…except Houston traded Largent before he ever played a game, dealing him to Seattle for an eighth-round draft pick. And the player Houston dealt, Lynn Dickey, became the Packers' starting quarterback for the next decade.

JAMES HARRIS (for more information, see pages 78–79)

YEAR	TEAM	G	ATT	COMP	PCT	YDS	YPA	TD	INT	RATING	RUSHING ATT	YDS	TD
1969	Buffalo	4	36	15	41.7	270	7.50	1	1	65.7	10	25	0
1970	Buffalo	7	50	24	48.0	338	6.76	3	4	56.9	3	-8	0
1971	Buffalo	7	103	51	49.5	512	4.97	1	6	43.0	6	42	0
1972						DID NOT PLAY							
1973	L.A. Rams	8	11	7	63.6	68	6.18	0	0	80.9	4	29	0
1974	L.A. Rams	11	198	106	53.5	1,544	7.80	11	6	85.1	42	112	5
1975	L.A. Rams	13	285	157	55.1	2,148	7.54	14	15	73.8	18	45	1
1976	L.A. Rams	7	158	91	57.6	1,460	9.24	8	6	89.6	12	76	2
1977	San Diego	9	211	109	51.7	1,240	5.88	5	11	55.8	10	13	2
1978	San Diego	9	88	42	47.7	518	5.89	2	9	34.4	10	7	0
1979	San Diego	8	9	5	55.6	38	4.22	0	1	26.4	6	26	0
Totals		83	1,149	607	52.8	8,136	7.08	45	59	67.3	121	367	10

Transactions

- Selected by Buffalo Bills in eighth round (192nd pick overall) of the 1969 NFL Draft;
- Released by Bills (Sept. 21, 1972); signed by Los Angeles Rams (Nov. 6, 1972);
- Traded by Rams to San Diego Chargers for fourth-round (DB Derwin Tucker) pick in the 1979 NFL Draft (June 14, 1977).

Noteworthy

- Selected to play in one Pro Bowl (following the 1974 season);
- Earned Pro Bowl player of the game honors in NFC's 17–10 victory;
- Led the NFC in passer rating (1976);
- From 1974–76, Rams posted a 20–6 record with Harris as the starting quarterback;
- Was first African-American quarterback to start a season opener (1969);
- In 1974, led Rams to a 7–2 record and became the first African-American quarterback to start (and win) a postseason game, as the Rams defeated the Washington Redskins 19–10 in a NFC Divisional Playoff Game;
- Completed 17 of 29 passes for a career-high 436 yards (25.6 yards per completion) and 2 touchdowns as the Rams overcame a 14–0 halftime deficit to defeat the Miami Dolphins 31–28 (at Miami, Oct. 3, 1976);
- Missed 1975 playoffs after suffering a bruised shoulder with two games left in the season;
- Also missed parts of the 1969, 1971, and 1976 seasons with injuries;
- Served as scout for the Tampa Bay Buccaneers (1986–1992) and assistant general manager for the New York Jets (1993–96);
- Earned a Super Bowl XXXV ring while serving as pro personnel director for the Baltimore Ravens (1997–2002);
- Hired as Jacksonville Jaguars' vice president of player personnel (2003);
- Played collegiately at Grambling State, where he guided the Tigers to consecutive conference titles (1967 and 1968) and was the most valuable player of the 1967 Orange Blossom Classic.

JIM HART (for more information, see pages 102–103)

YEAR	TEAM	G	ATT	COMP	PCT	YDS	YPA	TD	INT	RATING	RUSHING		
											ATT	YDS	TD
1966	St. Louis	1	11	4	36.4	29	2.64	0	0	44.9	0	0	0
1967	St. Louis	14	397	192	48.4	3,008	7.58	19	30	58.4	13	36	3
1968	St. Louis	13	316	140	44.3	2,059	6.52	15	18	58.2	19	20	6
1969	St. Louis	9	169	84	49.7	1,086	6.43	6	12	52.5	7	16	2
1970	St. Louis	14	373	171	45.8	2,575	6.90	14	18	61.5	18	18	0
1971	St. Louis	11	243	110	45.3	1,626	6.69	8	14	54.7	13	9	0
1972	St. Louis	6	119	60	50.4	857	7.20	5	5	70.6	9	17	0
1973	St. Louis	12	320	178	55.6	2,223	6.95	15	10	80.0	3	-3	0
1974	St. Louis	14	388*	200	51.5	2,411	6.21	20	8	79.5	10	21	2
1975	St. Louis	14	345	182	52.8	2,507	7.27	19	19	71.7	11	7	1
1976	St. Louis	14	388	218	56.2	2,946	7.59	18	13	82.0	8	7	0
1977	St. Louis	14	355	186	52.4	2,542	7.16	13	20	64.3	11	18	0
1978	St. Louis	15	477	240	50.3	3,121	6.54	16	18	66.7	11	11	2
1979	St. Louis	14	378	194	51.3	2,218	5.87	9	20	55.2	6	11	0
1980	St. Louis	15	425	228	53.6	2,946	6.93	16	20	68.6	9	11	0
1981	St. Louis	10	241	134	55.6	1,694	7.03	11	14	68.7	3	2	0
1982	St. Louis	4	33	19	57.6	199	6.03	1	0	85.3	0	0	0
1983	St. Louis	5	91	50	54.9	592	6.51	4	8	53.0	5	12	0
1984	Washington	2	7	3	42.9	26	3.71	0	0	53.3	3	-6	0
Totals		**201**	**5,076**	**2,593**	**51.1**	**34,665**	**6.83**	**209**	**247**	**66.6**	**159**	**207**	**16**

*Led league

Transactions
- Signed as an undrafted free agent by the St. Louis Cardinals (1966);
- Released by Cardinals, signed by Washington Redskins (Feb. 14, 1984).

Noteworthy
- Selected to four Pro Bowls (following the 1974–77 seasons);
- 1974 NFC player of the year;
- Set NFL mark for longest nonscoring pass, 98 yards to Bobby Moore (who later changed his name to Ahmad Rashad) (vs. Los Angeles Rams, Dec. 10, 1972);
- Owns Cardinals career records for: service (18 seasons); touchdown passes (209); passing yards (34,639); and completions (2,590);
- Although he was a record-setting passer at Southern Illinois, Hart was undrafted and played only one game as a rookie; he became the starter four days before his second season, 1967, when Charley Johnson was called into the Army;
- Bud Wilkinson, who coached the Cardinals in 1978 and 1979: "One of the most appealing things about going to the Cardinals was getting to work with a quarterback of the caliber of Jim Hart. I felt that he was one of the best passers, leaders, and overall quarterbacks in the game."

SONNY JURGENSEN (for more information, see pages 54–55)

YEAR	TEAM	G	ATT	COMP	PCT	YDS	YPA	TD	INT	RATING	ATT	YDS	TD
											RUSHING		
1957	Philadelphia	10	70	33	47.1	470	6.71	5	8	53.6	10	-3	2
1958	Philadelphia	12	22	12	54.5	259	11.77	0	1	77.7	1	1	0
1959	Philadelphia	12	5	3	60.0	27	5.40	1	0	114.2	0	0	0
1960	Philadelphia	12	44	24	54.5	486	11.05	5	1	122.0	4	5	0
1961	Philadelphia	14	416	235*	56.5	3,723*	8.95	32*	24	88.1	20	27	0
1962	Philadelphia	14	366	196	53.6	3,261*	8.91*	22	26	74.3	17	44	2
1963	Philadelphia	9	184	99	53.8	1,413	7.68	11	13	69.4	13	38	1
1964	Washington	14	385	207	53.8	2,934	7.62	24	13	85.4	27	57	3
1965	Washington	13	356	190	53.4	2,367	6.65	15	16	69.6	17	23	2
1966	Washington	14	436*	254*	58.3	3,209*	7.36	28	19	84.5	12	14	0
1967	Washington	14	508*	288*	56.7	3,747*	7.38	31*	16	87.3	15	46	2
1968	Washington	12	292	167	57.2	1,980	6.78	17	11	81.7	8	21	0
1969	Washington	14	442*	274*	62.0	3,102*	7.02	22	15	85.4	17	156	1
1970	Washington	14	337	202	59.9*	2,354	6.99	23	10	91.5	6	39	1
1971	Washington	5	28	16	57.1	170	6.07	0	2	45.2	3	29	0
1972	Washington	7	59	39	66.1	633	10.73	2	4	84.9	4	-5	0
1973	Washington	14	145	87	60.0	904	6.23	6	5	77.5	3	7	0
1974	Washington	14	167	107	64.1	1,185	7.10	11	5	94.5	4	-6	0
Totals		218	4,262	2,433	57.1	32,224	7.56	255	189	82.6	181	493	15

*Led league

Transactions

- Selected by Philadelphia Eagles in fourth round (43rd pick overall) of the 1957 NFL Draft;
- Traded with CB Jimmy Carr by Eagles to Washington Redskins for QB Norm Snead and CB Claude Crabb (April 1, 1964).

Noteworthy

- Inducted into Pro Football Hall of Fame in 1983;
- Selected to five Pro Bowls (following the 1961, 1964, 1966, 1967, and 1969 seasons);
- Completed record-tying 99-yard touchdown pass to Gerry Allen (vs. Chicago, Sept. 15, 1968);
- Was a backup to Norm Van Brocklin when the Eagles won the 1960 NFL Championship Game;
- Tied for first on NFL all-time list for seasons leading league in passing yards (5);
- Shares third place on NFL all-time list for seasons leading league in completions (4);
- Owns single-season record for touchdown passes for two different franchises (32 for Philadelphia in 1961, and 31 for Washington in 1967);
- Redskins career leader for: passer rating (85.0); completion percentage (58.0); and most consecutive games with a touchdown pass (23);
- In 1968, played the majority of the season with a protective vest to protect his fractured ribs;
- In 1971, injured his shoulder making a tackle in a preseason game and missed most of season;
- In 1972, tore his Achilles tendon and was unable to play in Super Bowl VII.

JIM KELLY (for more information, see pages 104–105)

YEAR	TEAM	G	ATT	COMP	PCT	YDS	YPA	TD	INT	RATING	Rushing ATT	YDS	TD
1984	Houston (USFL)	18	587*	370*	63.0	5,219*	8.89*	44*	26	98.2	85	493	
1985	Houston (USFL)	14	567*	360*	63.5*	4,623*	8.15	39*	19	97.9	28	170	
1986	Buffalo	16	480	285	59.4	3,593	7.49	22	17	83.3	41	199	
1987	Buffalo	12	419	250	59.7	2,798	6.68	19	11	83.8	29	133	
1988	Buffalo	16	452	269	59.5	3,380	7.48	15	17	78.2	35	154	
1989	Buffalo	13	391	228	58.3	3,130	8.01	25	18	86.2	29	137	
1990	Buffalo	14	346	219	63.3*	2,829	8.18	24	9	101.2*	22	63	
1991	Buffalo	15	474	304	64.1	3,844	8.11	33*	17	97.6	20	45	
1992	Buffalo	16	462	269	58.2	3,457	7.48	23	19	81.2	31	53	
1993	Buffalo	16	470	288	61.3	3,382	7.20	18	18	79.9	36	102	
1994	Buffalo	14	448	285	63.6	3,114	6.95	22	17	84.6	25	77	
1995	Buffalo	15	458	255	55.7	3,130	6.83	22	13	81.1	17	20	
1996	Buffalo	13	379	222	58.6	2,810	7.41	14	19	73.2	19	66	
NFL Totals		**160**	**4,779**	**2,874**	**60.1**	**35,467**	**7.42**	**237**	**175**	**84.4**	**304**	**1,049**	
USFL Totals		**32**	**1,154**	**730**	**63.3**	**9,842**	**8.53**	**83**	**45**	**98.1**	**113**	**663**	
Totals		**192**	**5,933**	**3,604**	**60.7**	**45,310**	**7.64**	**320**	**220**	**86.4**	**417**	**1,712**	

*Led league

Transactions
- Selected by Chicago Blitz in the 14th round (163rd overall pick) of the 1983 USFL Draft;
- Selected by Buffalo Bills in the first round (14th pick overall) of the 1983 NFL Draft;
- USFL rights traded by Blitz with RB Mark Rush to Houston Gamblers for four draft picks in the 1984 USFL Draft (June 9, 1983);
- Signed by Gamblers (June 9, 1983);
- Traded with 21 other players to New Jersey Generals for past considerations (March 7, 1986);
- Granted free agency when USFL suspended operations (Aug. 7, 1986);
- Signed by Bills (Aug. 18, 1986);
- On injured reserve with knee injury (Dec. 16–end of 1994 season).

Noteworthy
- Inducted into Pro Football Hall of Fame in 2002;
- Selected to four Pro Bowls (following the 1987 and 1990–92 seasons);
- Led Bills to four consecutive AFC titles (1990–93);
- Completed 18 of 30 passes for 212 yards in XXV;
- Completed 28 of 58 passes for 275 yards and 2 touchdowns in XXVI;
- Injured in second quarter of XXVII, but came back in XXVIII to complete 31 of 50 for 207 yards;
- Super Bowl single-game record holder for completions (31 in XXVIII) and attempts (58 in XXVI);
- His uniform number 12 was retired by the Bills;
- Bills career and single-season leader in passing yards, touchdowns, and completions.

BOBBY LAYNE (for more information, see pages 56–57)

YEAR	TEAM	G	ATT	COMP	PCT	YDS	YPA	TD	INT	RATING	RUSHING ATT	YDS	TD
948	Chicago Bears	11	52	16	30.8	232	4.46	3	2	49.5	13	80	1
949	N.Y. Bulldogs	12	299	155	51.8	1,796	6.01	9	18	55.3	54	196	3
950	Detroit	12	336*	152	45.2	2,323	6.91	16	18	62.1	56	250	4
951	Detroit	12	332*	152*	45.8	2,403*	7.24	26*	23	67.6	61	290	1
952	Detroit	12	287	139	48.4	1,999	6.97	19	20	64.5	94	411	1
953	Detroit	12	273	125	45.8	2,088	7.65	16	21	59.6	87	343	0
954	Detroit	12	246	135	54.9	1,818	7.39	14	12	77.3	30	119	2
955	Detroit	12	270	143	53.0	1,830	6.78	11	17	61.8	31	111	0
956	Detroit	12	244	129	52.9	1,909	7.82	9	17	62.0	46	169	5
957	Detroit	11	179	87	48.6	1,169	6.53	6	12	53.0	24	99	0
958	Detroit	2	26	12	46.2	171	6.58	1	2	48.7	3	1	0
958	Pittsburgh	10	268	133	49.6	2,339	8.73	13	10	80.4	37	153	3
959	Pittsburgh	12	297	142	47.8	1,986	6.69	20	21	62.8	33	181	2
960	Pittsburgh	12	209	103	49.3	1,814	8.68	13	17	66.2	19	12	2
961	Pittsburgh	8	149	75	50.3	1,205	8.09	11	16	62.8	8	11	0
962	Pittsburgh	13	233	116	49.8	1,686	7.24	9	17	56.2	15	25	1
Totals		**175**	**3,700**	**1,814**	**49.0**	**26,768**	**7.23**	**196**	**243**	**63.4**	**611**	**2,451**	**25**

Led league

Transactions

- Selected by Chicago Bears in first round (third pick overall) of the 1948 NFL Draft;
- Traded by Bears to N.Y. Bulldogs for $50,000 cash (1949);
- Traded by Bulldogs to Lions for WR Bob Mann and $37,500 cash (1950);
- Traded by Lions to Pittsburgh Steelers for QB Earl Morrall and second- (T Mike Rabold) and sixth-round (T Dick Guesman) picks of the 1959 NFL Draft (Oct. 6, 1958).

Noteworthy

- Inducted into Pro Football Hall of Fame in 1967;
- Selected to six Pro Bowls (following the 1951–53, 1956, 1958, and 1959 seasons);
- Starting quarterback for Detroit Lions' 1952 and 1953 NFL Championship Game victories;
- Was on team but injured when Lions won 1957 NFL title;
- In the 1953 NFL Championship Game, guided team 80 yards, capped by a 33-yard touchdown pass with 2:08 remaining, to give Lions a 17–16 victory and NFL title;
- Lions career record holder for: passing yards (15,710); touchdowns (118); and completions (1,074);
- Steelers single-game record holder for passing yards (409 vs. Chicago Cardinals, Dec. 13, 1958);
- Served as backup to future Pro Football Hall of Fame Sid Luckman his rookie season;
- Did not lose a game in three seasons as a college baseball pitcher at Texas;
- Lions teammate, running back Doak Walker: "Bobby never lost a game in his life. Once in a while time ran out on him."

SID LUCKMAN (for more information, see pages 80–81)

YEAR	TEAM	G	ATT	COMP	PCT	YDS	YPA	TD	INT	RATING	RUSHING ATT	YDS	TD
1939	Chicago Bears	11	51	23	45.1	636	12.47*	5	4	91.6	24	42	(
1940	Chicago Bears	11	105	48	45.7	941	8.96*	4	9	54.5	23	-65	(
1941	Chicago Bears	11	119	68	57.1*	1,181	9.92*	9	6	95.3	18	18	
1942	Chicago Bears	11	105	57	54.3	1,024	9.75	10	13	80.1	13	-6	(
1943	Chicago Bears	10	202	110	54.5	2,194*	10.86*	28*	12	107.5	22	-40	
1944	Chicago Bears	7	143	71	49.7	1,018	7.12	11	12	63.8	20	-96	
1945	Chicago Bears	10	217	117	53.9	1,727*	7.96	14*	10	82.5	36	-118	
1946	Chicago Bears	11	229	110	48.0	1,826*	7.97	17*	16	71.0	25	-76	(
1947	Chicago Bears	12	323	176	54.5	2,712	8.40	24	31	67.7	10	86	
1948	Chicago Bears	12	163	89	54.6	1,047	6.42	13	14	65.1	8	11	(
1949	Chicago Bears	11	50	22	44.0	200	4.00	1	3	37.1	3	4	
1950	Chicago Bears	11	37	13	35.1	180	4.86	1	2	38.1	2	1	(
Totals		**128**	**1,744**	**904**	**51.8**	**14,686**	**8.42**	**137**	**132**	**75.0**	**204**	**-239**	**4**

*Led league

Transactions
• Selected by Chicago Bears in the first round (second pick overall) of the 1939 NFL Draft.

Noteworthy
• Inducted into Pro Football Hall of Fame in 1965;
• Selected to three Pro Bowls (following the 1940–42 seasons—the Pro Bowl was not played for the 1943–49 seasons);
• 1943 NFL most valuable player;
• Led Bears to 1940, 1941, 1943, and 1946 NFL Championship Games;
• Completed 5 touchdown passes in 1943 NFL Championship Game victory, a postseason mark that stood for a quarter century;
• Holds NFL record for most seasons leading league in yards per attempt (7), and for most consecutive seasons leading league in yards per attempt (5);
• Second in NFL career history in yards per attempt average (8.42);
• Second in NFL single-season history in yards per attempt average (10.86 in 1943);
• His uniform number 42 was retired by the Bears;
• With Luckman running the offense, Bears led the NFL in scoring four of his first five seasons;
• An all-around talent, Luckman played defense and had 17 career interceptions, including 2 he returned for touchdowns;
• Also was Bears' main punter for most his career, finishing with 230 punts for a 38.6 average;
• Attended college at New York City's Columbia University…in 1943, the N.Y. Giants hosted the Bears and honored the opposing quarterback (and sold a few extra seats) by promoting the game as "Sid Luckman Day," and Luckman responded by passing for a record 7 touchdown passes as Chicago defeated the Giants 56–7. The record has not been surpassed.

PEYTON MANNING (for more information, see pages 106–107)

YEAR	TEAM	G	ATT	COMP	PCT	YDS	YPA	TD	INT	RATING	RUSHING		
											ATT	YDS	TD
1998	Indianapolis	16	575*	326	56.7	3,739	6.50	26	28	71.2	15	62	0
1999	Indianapolis	16	533	331	62.1	4,135	7.76	26	15	90.7	35	73	2
2000	Indianapolis	16	571	357*	62.5	4,413	7.73	33*	15	94.7	37	116	1
2001	Indianapolis	16	547	343	62.7	4,131	7.55	26	23	84.1	35	157	4
2002	Indianapolis	16	591	392	66.3	4,200	7.11	27	19	88.8	38	148	2
Totals		**80**	**2,817**	**1,749**	**62.1**	**20,618**	**7.32**	**138**	**100**	**85.9**	**160**	**556**	**9**

*Led league

Transactions
• Selected by Indianapolis Colts in first round (first pick overall) of the 1998 NFL Draft.

Noteworthy
• Selected to three Pro Bowls (following the 1999, 2000, and 2002 seasons);
• Only quarterback in NFL history with 4,000 passing yards in four consecutive seasons;
• Holds NFL rookie season records for touchdown passes (26) and completions (326);
• Tied for most consecutive seasons with at least 25 touchdown passes (5);
• With every game he starts, Manning extends his NFL mark for most consecutive starts to begin a career by an NFL quarterback. The streak is at 80 games entering the 2003 season;
• Second-fastest player to reach 20,000 passing yards (78 games);
• Third-fastest player to reach 100 career touchdown passes (56 games);
• Owns five-best season passing yardage and completion totals in Colts history;
• First in Colts single-season annals in touchdown passes (33 in 2000);
• First in Colts history in career completion percentage (62.1);
• Peyton's father, Archie, was a first-round pick of the New Orleans Saints in 1971 and played quarterback for 14 NFL seasons (1971–1982 Saints, 1982 and 1983 Houston Oilers, and 1983 and 1984 Minnesota Vikings).

DAN MARINO (for more information, see pages 108–109)

YEAR	TEAM	G	ATT	COMP	PCT	YDS	YPA	TD	INT	RATING	RUSHING ATT	YDS	TD
1983	Miami	11	296	173	58.4	2,210	7.47	20	6	96.0	28	45	2
1984	Miami	16	564*	362*	64.2	5,084*	9.01*	48*	17	108.9*	28	-7	0
1985	Miami	16	567	336*	59.3	4,137*	7.30	30*	21	84.1	26	-24	0
1986	Miami	16	623*	378*	60.7	4,476*	7.62	44*	23	92.5	12	-3	0
1987	Miami	12	444	263	59.2	3,245	7.31	26	13	89.2	12	-5	1
1988	Miami	16	606*	354*	58.4	4,434*	7.32	28	23	80.8	20	-17	0
1989	Miami	16	550	308	56.0	3,997	7.27	24	22	76.9	14	-7	2
1990	Miami	16	531	306	57.6	3,563	6.71	21	11	82.6	16	29	0
1991	Miami	16	554*	330*	59.6	4,116*	7.43	24	16	85.1	27	32	1
1992	Miami	16	554*	330*	59.6	4,116*	7.43	24	16	85.1	20	66	0
1993	Miami	5	150	91	60.7	1,218	8.12	8	3	95.9	9	-4	1
1994	Miami	16	615	385	62.6	4,453	7.24	30	17	89.2	22	-6	1
1995	Miami	14	482	309	64.1	3,668	7.61	24	15	90.8	11	14	0
1996	Miami	13	373	221	59.2	2,795	7.49	17	9	87.7	11	-3	0
1997	Miami	16	548*	319*	58.2	3,780	6.90	16	11	80.7	18	-14	0
1998	Miami	16	537	310	57.7	3,497	6.51	23	15	80.0	21	-3	1
1999	Miami	11	369	204	55.3	2,448	6.63	12	17	67.4	6	-6	0
Totals		**242**	**8,358***	**4,967***	**59.4**	**61,361***	**7.34**	**420***	**252**	**86.4**	**301**	**87**	**9**

*Led league

Transactions
- Selected by Los Angeles Express in the first round (first pick overall) of the 1983 USFL Draft, but never played in USFL;
- Selected by Dolphins in the first round (27th pick overall) of the 1983 NFL Draft;
- On injured reserve with Achilles tendon injury (Oct. 13–end of 1993 season).

Noteworthy
- Selected to nine Pro Bowls (following the 1983–87, 1991, 1992, 1994, and 1995 seasons);
- Led Dolphins to 1984 AFC title and berth in Super Bowl XIX;
- Completed 29 of 50 passes for 318 yards and 1 touchdown in XIX;
- His uniform number 13 was retired by the Dolphins;
- NFL career leader in: passing yards (61,361); touchdown passes (420); completions (4,967); most 3,000-yard passing seasons (13); most 20-touchdown seasons (13); most seasons leading league in completions (6); most 400-yard passing games (13); most 300-yard passing games (63); most 4-touchdown games (21); and most consecutive games with at least 4 touchdown passes (4);
- NFL single-season record holder for: passing yards (5,084 in 1984); touchdown passes (48 in 1984); highest rookie passer rating (96.0 in 1983); highest rookie completion percentage (58.4 in 1983); most 400-yard passing games (4 in 1984); and most 4-touchdown games (6 in 1984);
- Led Dolphins to 37 fourth-quarter comeback victories, most in NFL history.

JIM McMAHON (for more information, see pages 58–59)

EAR	TEAM	G	ATT	COMP	PCT	YDS	YPA	TD	INT	RATING	RUSHING ATT	RUSHING YDS	RUSHING TD
'82	Chicago	8	210	120	57.1	1,504	7.15	9	7	79.9	24	105	1
'83	Chicago	14	295	175	59.3	2,184	7.40	12	13	77.6	55	307	2
'84	Chicago	9	143	85	59.4	1,146	8.01	8	2	97.8	39	276	2
'85	Chicago	13	313	178	56.9	2,392	7.64	15	11	82.6	47	252	3
'86	Chicago	6	150	77	51.3	995	6.63	5	8	61.4	22	152	1
'87	Chicago	7	210	125	59.5	1,639	7.80	12	8	87.4	22	88	2
'88	Chicago	9	192	114	59.4	1,346	7.01	6	7	76.0	26	104	4
'89	San Diego	12	318	176	55.3	2,132	6.70	10	10	73.5	29	141	0
'90	Philadelphia	5	9	6	66.7	63	7.00	0	0	86.8	3	1	0
'91	Philadelphia	12	311	187	60.1	2,239	7.20	12	11	80.3	22	55	1
'92	Philadelphia	4	43	212	51.2	279	6.49	1	2	60.1	6	23	0
'93	Minnesota	12	331	200	60.4	1,968	5.95	9	8	76.2	33	96	0
'94	Arizona	2	43	23	53.5	219	5.09	1	3	46.6	6	32	0
'95	Green Bay	1	1	1	100.0	6	6.00	0	0	91.7	0	0	0
'96	Green Bay	5	4	3	75.0	39	9.75	0	0	105.2	4	-1	0
tals		**119**	**2,573**	**1,492**	**58.0**	**18,148**	**7.05**	**100**	**90**	**78.2**	**338**	**1,631**	**16**

ansactions

Selected by Chicago Bears in the first round (fifth pick overall) of the 1982 NFL Draft;
On injured reserve with lacerated kidney (Nov. 9–end of 1984 season);
On injured reserve with shoulder injury (Nov. 28–end of 1986 season);
On injured reserve with shoulder injury (Sept. 7–Oct. 22, 1987);
On injured reserve with knee injury (Nov. 5–Dec. 9, 1988);
Traded by Bears to San Diego Chargers for second-round pick (LB Ron Cox) in 1990 NFL Draft (Aug. 18, 1989);
Granted free agency, signed by Philadelphia Eagles (July 10, 1990);
Granted unconditional free agency, signed by Minnesota Vikings (March 30, 1993);
Released by Vikings (March 14, 1994), signed by Arizona Cardinals (June 2, 1994);
Granted unconditional free agency, signed by Cleveland Browns (Aug. 8, 1995);
Claimed on waivers by Green Bay Packers (Nov. 28, 1995).

oteworthy

Selected to one Pro Bowl (following the 1985 season);
Starting quarterback for Bears' Super Bowl XX victory;
Completed 12 of 20 passes for 256 yards and ran for 2 touchdowns in Super Bowl XX;
Posted a .691 winning percentage (67–30) as starting quarterback;
Earned second ring as backup quarterback for Super Bowl XXXI champion Packers;
Had 5 career receptions, including 2 touchdown catches, and punted twice for 47.5 average;
Set 70 NCAA Division I passing and total offense records while at Brigham Young University.

DONOVAN McNABB (for more information, see pages 36–37)

YEAR	TEAM	G	ATT	COMP	PCT	YDS	YPA	TD	INT	RATING	RUSHING ATT	YDS	TD
1999	Philadelphia	12	216	106	49.1	948	4.39	8	7	60.1	47	313	
2000	Philadelphia	16	569	330	58.0	3,365	5.91	21	13	77.8	86	629	
2001	Philadelphia	16	493	285	57.8	3,233	6.56	25	12	84.3	82	482	
2002	Philadelphia	10	361	211	58.4	2,289	6.34	17	6	86.0	63	460	
Totals		**54**	**1,639**	**932**	**56.9**	**9,835**	**6.00**	**71**	**38**	**79.2**	**278**	**1,884**	**1**

Transactions
• Selected by Philadelphia Eagles in the first round (second pick overall) of the 1999 NFL Draft.

Noteworthy
• Selected to three Pro Bowls (following the 2000–2002 seasons);
• Led Eagles to NFC Championship Game (2000 and 2002);
• Owns a .646 winning percentage (31–17) as a starter;
• Fourth on NFL all-time list for touchdown-to-interception ratio (1.86);
• Most rushing yards by a quarterback after four seasons;
• Eagles postseason leader in completions (150) and passing yards (1,459);
• Injured his ankle on the third play of game against Arizona, but stayed in the game and passed for 225 yards and 4 touchdowns; after the game, it was discovered the ankle was broken (Nov. 17, 2002);
• First quarterback with two 100-yard rushing games in the same season since 1972 (2002);
• Just fifth quarterback since 1970 to rush for a touchdown in four consecutive games (2002);
• In his first full season as starter, finished second in the league's MVP voting (2000);
• Fifth-most rushing yards in a season by a quarterback (629 in 2000);
• His 7.3-yard rushing average in 2002 was the highest of any player with at least 50 attempts;
• He plays his best at night: in seven career prime-time games, has a 7–0 record and sterling 94.7 passer rating;
• Owns Eagles single-season record for attempts and completions;
• Backup guard on two Syracuse basketball teams, including the 1995–96 team that lost to Kentucky in the NCAA championship game;
• At Mount Carmel High School, was a football teammate of Simeon Rice and a basketball teammate of Antoine Walker.

STEVE McNAIR (for more information, see pages 38–39)

Year	Team	G	Att	Comp	Pct	Yds	YPA	TD	Int	Rating	Rushing Att	Yds	TD
1995	Houston	4	80	41	51.3	569	7.11	3	1	81.7	11	38	0
1996	Houston	9	143	88	61.5	1,197	8.37	6	4	90.6	31	169	2
1997	Tennessee	16	415	216	52.0	2,665	6.42	14	13	70.4	101	674	8
1998	Tennessee	16	492	289	58.7	3,228	6.56	15	10	80.1	77	559	4
1999	Tennessee	11	331	187	56.5	2,179	6.58	12	8	78.6	72	337	8
2000	Tennessee	16	396	248	62.6	2,847	7.19	15	13	83.2	72	403	0
2001	Tennessee	15	431	264	61.3	3,350	7.77	21	12	90.2	75	414	5
2002	Tennessee	16	492	301	61.2	3,387	6.88	22	15	84.0	82	440	3
Totals		**103**	**2,780**	**1,634**	**58.8**	**19,422**	**6.99**	**108**	**76**	**81.7**	**521**	**3,034**	**30**

Transactions

• Selected by Houston Oilers in the first round (third pick overall) of the 1995 NFL Draft; Oilers franchise moved to Tennessee in 1997 and renamed Titans in 1999.

Noteworthy

• Starting quarterback for Titans in Super Bowl XXXIV;
• Completed 22 of 36 passes for 214 yards and rushed for team-high 64 yards in XXXIV; Also guided Titans to the 2002 AFC Championship Game;
• Fifth player in NFL history to pass for 18,000 yards and rush for more than 3,000 yards;
• Owns a .621 winning percentage (59–36) as a starter;
• Second-best single-season passer rating in club history (90.2 in 2001);
Missed five games because of back surgery in 1999, but returned to Titans in late October and guided the franchise to its first Super Bowl appearance;
In 1999 AFC Championship Game against Jacksonville, passed for 112 yards and 1 touchdown and rushed for 91 yards and 2 touchdowns;
Did not practice most of the final two months of 2002 season, but never missed a game and led Titans to AFC Championship Game;
Senior season at Alcorn State, won the 1994 Walter Payton Award (top Division I-AA player) and finished third in the Heisman Trophy voting;
Only player in NCAA history to gain more than 16,000 total yards in his career;
Set overall NCAA record with 8.18 yards gained per pass play;
Drafted by baseball's Seattle Mariners coming out of high school;
A great two-way player in high school, tied Mississippi's state record by intercepting 30 passes as a defensive back in his career.

DON MEREDITH <small>(for more information, see pages 60–61)</small>

YEAR	TEAM	G	ATT	COMP	PCT	YDS	YPA	TD	INT	RATING	RUSHING ATT	YDS	TD
1960	Dallas	6	68	29	42.6	281	4.13	2	5	34.0	3	4	
1961	Dallas	8	182	94	51.6	1,161	6.38	9	11	63.0	22	176	
1962	Dallas	13	212	105	49.5	1,679	7.92	15	8	84.2	21	74	
1963	Dallas	14	310	167	53.9	2,381	7.68	17	18	73.1	41	185	
1964	Dallas	12	323	158	48.9	2,143	6.63	9	16	59.1	32	81	
1965	Dallas	14	305	141	46.2	2,415	7.92	22	13	79.9	35	247	
1966	Dallas	13	344	177	51.5	2,805	8.15	24	12	87.7	38	242	
1967	Dallas	11	255	128	50.2	1,834	7.19	16	16	68.7	28	84	
1968	Dallas	13	309	171	55.3	2,500	8.09	21	12	88.4	22	123	
Totals		**104**	**2,308**	**1,170**	**50.7**	**17,199**	**7.45**	**135**	**111**	**74.8**	**242**	**1,216**	

Transactions
- Selected by Chicago Bears in the third round (32nd pick overall) of the 1960 NFL Draft;
- Traded by Bears to Dallas Cowboys for third-round pick (WR Jim Bates) in 1962 NFL Draft (1960).

Noteworthy
- Selected to three Pro Bowls (following the 1966–68 seasons);
- Guided Cowboys to first three playoff appearances (1966–68);
- Inducted into Cowboys' Ring of Honor (1976);
- Only Cowboys quarterback with four 3-touchdown games in a season (1966);
- Only Cowboys quarterback to post consecutive 300-yard passing games (1963);
- Completed longest pass in Cowboys history (95 yards to Bob Hayes, Nov. 13, 1966);
- Owns the top three single-game marks for highest average gain per pass attempt;
- Played through a plethora of injuries: shoulder separation in 1961; hand injury in 1962; knee-ankle-shoulder-stomach problems in 1964; arm injury in 1965; and rib injury in 1967;
- Cowboys coach Tom Landry once remarked, "I don't understand how Meredith can come back from something like that";
- Cowboys founder Clint Murchison Jr. signed Meredith to a personal services contract before Dallas was awarded an NFL franchise; the Bears drafted Meredith, and then, after the Cowboy franchise was founded, dealt him to Dallas;
- Set an NCAA record by completing 61 percent of his passes at Southern Methodist University;
- Served 12 years as commentator on ABC's *NFL Monday Night Football* (1970–73, 1977–1984);
- Nicknamed "Dandy Don," as a broadcaster Meredith would sing "Turn out the lights, the par over" when he felt a team had a safe lead.

JOE MONTANA

(for more information, see pages 16–17)

YEAR	TEAM	G	ATT	COMP	PCT	YDS	YPA	TD	INT	RATING	RUSHING ATT	YDS	TD
1979	San Francisco	16	23	13	56.5	96	4.17	1	0	81.1	3	22	0
1980	San Francisco	15	273	176	64.5*	1,795	6.58	15	9	87.8	32	77	2
1981	San Francisco	16	488	311	63.7*	3,565	7.31	19	12	88.4	25	95	2
1982	San Francisco	9	346*	213	61.6	2,613	7.55	17*	11	88.0	30	118	1
1983	San Francisco	16	515	332	64.5	3,910	7.59	26	12	94.6	61	284	2
1984	San Francisco	16	432	279	64.6	3,630	8.40	28	10	102.9	39	118	2
1985	San Francisco	15	494	303	61.3*	3,653	7.39	27	13	91.3	42	153	3
1986	San Francisco	8	307	191	62.2	2,236	7.28	8	9	80.7	17	38	0
1987	San Francisco	13	398	266	66.8*	3,054	7.67	31*	13	102.1*	35	141	1
1988	San Francisco	14	397	238	59.9	2,981	7.51	18	10	87.9	38	132	3
1989	San Francisco	13	386	271	70.2*	3,521	9.12*	26	8	112.4*	49	227	3
1990	San Francisco	15	520	321	61.7	3,944	7.58	26	16	89.0	40	162	1
1991	San Francisco				DID NOT PLAY								
1992	San Francisco	1	21	15	71.4	126	6.00	2	0	118.4	3	28	0
1993	Kansas City	11	298	181	60.7	2,144	7.19	13	7	87.4	25	64	0
1994	Kansas City	14	493	299	60.6	3,283	6.66	16	9	83.6	18	17	0
Totals		**192**	**5,391**	**3,409**	**63.2**	**40,551**	**7.52**	**273**	**139**	**92.3**	**457**	**1,676**	**20**

*Led league

Transactions
- Selected by San Francisco 49ers in the third round (82nd overall pick) of the 1979 NFL Draft;
- On injured reserve with back injury (Sept. 15–Nov. 6, 1986);
- On injured reserve with elbow injury (Aug. 27–end of 1991 season);
- On injured reserve with elbow injury (Sept. 1–Dec. 18, 1992);
- Traded by 49ers with S David Whitmore and third-round pick (WR Lake Dawson) in 1994 NFL Draft to Kansas City Chiefs for first-round pick (traded) in 1993 NFL Draft.

Noteworthy
- Inducted into Pro Football Hall of Fame in 2000;
- Selected to eight Pro Bowls (following the 1981, 1983–85, 1987, 1989, 1990, and 1993 seasons);
- Starting quarterback in 49ers' Super Bowl victories in XVI, XIX, XXIII, and XXIV;
- Completed 14 of 22 passes for 157 yards and 1 touchdown and was named MVP of XVI;
- Completed 24 of 35 passes for 331 yards and 3 touchdowns and was named MVP of XIX;
- Completed 23 of 36 passes for 357 yards and 2 touchdowns in XXIII;
- Completed 22 of 29 passes for 297 yards and 5 touchdowns and was named MVP of XXIV;
- His uniform number 16 was retired by the 49ers;
- Engineered game-winning 92-yard touchdown drive, capped by 10-yard touchdown pass to John Taylor with 34 seconds remaining, to win XXIII;
- Holds Super Bowl records for: passer rating (127.8); completions (83); consecutive completions (13); passing yards (1,142); touchdown passes (11).

WARREN MOON (for more information, see pages 110–111)

Year	Team	G	Att	Comp	Pct	Yds	YPA	TD	Int	Rating	Rushing Att	Yds	TD
1978	Edmonton (CFL)	16	173	89	51.4	1,112	6.43	5	7	—	30	114	1
1979	Edmonton (CFL)	16	274	149	54.4	2,382	8.69	20	12	—	56	150	2
1980	Edmonton (CFL)	16	331	181	54.7	3,127	9.45	25	11	98.3	55	352	3
1981	Edmonton (CFL)	15	378	237	62.7	3,959	10.47	27	12	108.6	50	298	3
1982	Edmonton (CFL)	16	562	333	59.3	5,000	8.90	36	16	98.0	54	259	4
1983	Edmonton (CFL)	16	664	380	57.2	5,648	8.51	31	19	88.9	85	527	3
1984	Houston	16	450	259	57.6	3,338	7.42	12	14	76.9	58	211	1
1985	Houston	14	377	200	53.1	2,709	7.19	15	19	68.5	39	130	0
1986	Houston	15	488	256	52.5	3,489	7.15	13	26	62.3	42	157	2
1987	Houston	12	368	184	50.0	2,806	7.63	21	18	74.2	34	112	3
1988	Houston	11	294	160	54.4	2,327	7.91	17	8	88.4	33	88	5
1989	Houston	16	464	280	60.3	3,631	7.83	23	14	88.9	70	268	4
1990	Houston	15	584*	362*	62.0	4,689*	8.03	33*	13	96.8	55	215	2
1991	Houston	16	655*	404*	61.7	4,690*	7.16	23	21	81.7	33	68	2
1992	Houston	11	346	224	64.7	2,521	7.29	18	12	89.3	27	147	1
1993	Houston	15	520	303	58.3	3,485	6.70	21	21	75.2	48	145	1
1994	Minnesota	15	601	371	61.7	4,264	7.09	18	19	79.9	27	55	0
1995	Minnesota	16	606	377*	62.2	4,228	6.98	33	14	91.5	33	82	0
1996	Minnesota	8	247	134	54.3	1,610	6.52	7	9	68.7	9	6	0
1997	Seattle	15	528	313	59.3	3,678	6.97	25	16	83.7	17	40	1
1998	Seattle	10	258	145	56.2	1,632	6.33	11	8	76.6	16	10	0
1999	Kansas City	1	3	1	33.3	20	6.67	0	0	57.6	0	0	0
2000	Kansas City	2	34	15	44.1	208	6.12	1	1	61.9	2	2	0
NFL Totals		**208**	**6,823**	**3,988**	**58.4**	**49,325**	**7.23**	**291**	**233**	**80.9**	**543**	**1,736**	**22**
CFL Totals		**95**	**2,382**	**1,369**	**57.5**	**21,228**	**8.91**	**144**	**77**	**—**	**330**	**1,700**	**16**
Totals		**303**	**9,205**	**5,357**	**58.2**	**70,553**	**7.66**	**435**	**310**	**—**	**873**	**3,436**	**38**

*Led league

Transactions
- Signed by Edmonton Eskimos of CFL (March 1978);
- Granted free agency, signed by Houston Oilers (March 1, 1984);
- Injured reserve with fractured scapula (Sept. 5-Oct. 15, 1988);
- Traded by Oilers to Minnesota Vikings for third-round pick (WR Malcolm Seabron) in the 1994 NFL Draft and third-round pick (RB Rodney Thomas) in 1995 NFL Draft (April 14, 1994);
- Released by Vikings, signed by Seattle Seahawks (March 7, 1997);
- Released by Seahawks, signed by Kansas City Chiefs (April 27, 1999).

Noteworthy
- Selected to nine Pro Bowls (following the 1988–1995, and 1997 seasons);
- Most combined passing yards and touchdown passes in pro football history.

JOE NAMATH (for more information, see pages 62–63)

YEAR	TEAM	G	ATT	COMP	PCT	YDS	YPA	TD	INT	RATING	RUSHING ATT	YDS	TD
1965	N.Y. Jets	13	340	164	48.2	2,220	6.53	18	15	68.8	8	19	0
1966	N.Y. Jets	14	471*	232*	49.3	3,379*	7.17	19	27	62.6	6	42	2
1967	N.Y. Jets	14	491*	258*	52.5	4,007*	8.16*	26	28	73.8	6	14	0
1968	N.Y. Jets	14	380	187	49.2	3,147	8.28	15	17	72.1	5	11	2
1969	N.Y. Jets	14	361	185	51.2	2,734	7.57	19	17	74.3	11	33	2
1970	N.Y. Jets	5	179	90	50.3	1,259	7.03	5	12	54.7	1	-1	0
1971	N.Y. Jets	4	59	28	47.5	537	9.10	5	6	68.2	3	-1	0
1972	N.Y. Jets	13	324	162	50.0	2,816*	8.69	19*	21	72.5	6	8	0
1973	N.Y. Jets	6	133	68	51.1	966	7.26	5	6	68.7	1	-2	0
1974	N.Y. Jets	14	361	191	52.9	2,616	7.25	20	22	69.4	8	1	1
1975	N.Y. Jets	14	326	157	48.2	2,286	7.01	15	28	51.0	10	6	0
1976	N.Y. Jets	11	230	114	49.6	1,090	4.74	4	16	39.9	2	5	0
1977	Los Angeles	4	107	50	46.7	606	5.66	3	5	54.5	4	5	0
Totals		**140**	**3,762**	**1,886**	**50.1**	**27,663**	**7.35**	**173**	**220**	**65.5**	**71**	**140**	**7**

Led league

Transactions
• Selected by New York Jets in first round (first overall pick) of the 1965 AFL Draft;
• Released by Jets (1977), signed as free agent with Los Angeles Rams (April 2, 1977).

Noteworthy
• Inducted into Pro Football Hall of Fame in 1985;
• Selected to five Pro Bowls (following the 1965, 1967–69, and 1972 seasons);
• Chosen as the quarterback on the all-time AFL team;
• 1965 AFL rookie of the year;
• 1968 AFL player of the year;
• 1974 NFL comeback player of the year;
• Starting quarterback for Jets in Super Bowl III victory;
• Completed 17 of 28 passes for 206 yards and won MVP in Super Bowl III;
• Had predicted the Jets' victory a few days before the game; the win showed the football world that AFL teams were worthy of competing against the NFL;
• His uniform number 12 was retired by the Jets;
• First passer to pass for 4,000 yards in a season (4,007 in 1967)—a feat unmatched for 12 years;
• Owns Jets records for passing yards in a career (27,057), season (4,007), and game (496, on just 15 completions, at Baltimore Colts on Sept. 24, 1972);
• The AFL and NFL were in a fierce bidding war for players when Namath was drafted in 1965; one of the men who recruited him to sign with the Jets was assistant coach Chuck Knox. Twelve years later Knox was Namath's head coach for his final season;
• Nicknamed Broadway Joe because of his charisma and flair for the limelight, Namath also appeared in many movies and television shows.

JIM PLUNKETT (for more information, see pages 18–19)

YEAR	TEAM	G	ATT	COMP	PCT	YDS	YPA	TD	INT	RATING	RUSHING ATT	YDS	TD
1971	New England	14	328	158	48.2	2,158	6.58	19	16	68.6	45	210	
1972	New England	14	355	169	47.6	2,196	6.19	8	25	45.7	36	230	
1973	New England	14	376	193	51.3	2,550	6.78	13	17	65.8	44	209	
1974	New England	14	352	173	49.1	2,457	6.98	19	22	64.1	30	161	
1975	New England	5	92	36	39.1	571	6.21	3	7	39.7	4	7	
1976	San Francisco	12	243	126	51.9	1,592	6.55	13	16	63.0	19	95	
1977	San Francisco	14	248	128	51.6	1,693	6.83	9	14	62.1	28	71	
1978	Oakland					DID NOT PLAY							
1979	Oakland	4	15	7	46.7	89	5.93	1	1	60.1	3	18	
1980	Oakland	13	320	165	51.6	2,299	7.18	18	16	72.9	28	141	
1981	Oakland	9	179	94	52.5	1,045	5.84	4	9	56.7	12	38	
1982	L.A. Raiders	9	261	152	58.2	2,035	7.80	14	15	77.0	15	6	
1983	L.A. Raiders	14	379	230	60.7	2,935	7.74	20	18	82.7	26	78	
1984	L.A. Raiders	8	198	108	54.5	1,473	7.44	6	10	67.6	16	14	
1985	L.A. Raiders	3	103	71	68.9	803	7.80	3	3	89.6	5	12	
1986	L.A. Raiders	10	252	133	52.8	1,986	7.88	14	9	82.5	12	47	
Totals		**157**	**3,701**	**1,943**	**52.5**	**25,882**	**6.99**	**164**	**198**	**67.5**	**323**	**1,337**	

Transactions
- Selected by New England Patriots in the first round (first overall pick) of the 1971 NFL Draft;
- Traded by Patriots to San Francisco 49ers for QB Tom Owen and two first-round (C Pete Brock and S Tim Fox), selections in the 1976 NFL Draft, and first- (CB Raymond Clayborn) and secon round (RB Horace Ivory) picks in the 1977 NFL Draft;
- Released by 49ers (Aug. 28, 1978), signed by Oakland Raiders (Sept. 12, 1978);
- Raiders franchise moved to Los Angeles (1982);
- Injured reserve with pulled abdominal muscle (Oct. 13–Nov. 11, 1984);
- Injured reserve with dislocated shoulder (Sept. 23–end of 1985 season).

Noteworthy
- 1971 AFC rookie of the year;
- 1980 NFL comeback player of the year;
- Starting quarterback in Raiders' Super Bowl XV and XVIII victories;
- Completed 13 of 21 passes for 261 yards and 3 touchdowns and was named MVP of XV;
- Completed 16 of 25 passes for 172 yards and 1 touchdown in XVIII;
- Completed NFL record-tying 99-yard pass to Cliff Branch (vs. Washington, Oct. 2, 1983);
- Second-best passer rating in Super Bowl history (122.8);
- Attempted 46 Super Bowl passes without an interception, second-most attempts without havir thrown a Super Bowl interception;
- 1970 Heisman Trophy winner at Stanford;
- First Hispanic quarterback to win the Super Bowl.

PHIL SIMMS (for more information, see pages 112–113)

YEAR	TEAM	G	ATT	COMP	PCT	YDS	YPA	TD	INT	RATING	Rushing ATT	YDS	TD
1979	N.Y. Giants	12	265	134	50.6	1,743	6.58	13	14	66.0	29	166	1
1980	N.Y. Giants	13	402	193	48.0	2,321	5.77	15	19	58.9	36	190	1
1981	N.Y. Giants	10	316	172	54.4	2,031	6.43	11	9	74.0	19	42	0
1982	N.Y. Giants					DID NOT PLAY-INJURED							
1983	N.Y. Giants	2	13	7	53.8	130	10.00	0	1	56.6	0	0	0
1984	N.Y. Giants	16	533	286	53.7	4,044	7.59	22	18	78.1	42	162	0
1985	N.Y. Giants	16	495	275	55.6	3,829	7.74	22	20	78.6	37	132	0
1986	N.Y. Giants	16	468	259	55.3	3,487	7.45	21	22	74.6	43	72	1
1987	N.Y. Giants	9	282	163	57.8	2,230	7.91	17	9	90.0	14	44	0
1988	N.Y. Giants	15	479	263	54.9	3,359	7.01	21	11	82.1	33	152	0
1989	N.Y. Giants	15	405	228	56.3	3,061	7.56	14	14	77.6	32	141	0
1990	N.Y. Giants	14	311	184	59.2	2,284	7.34	15	4	92.7	21	61	1
1991	N.Y. Giants	6	141	82	58.2	993	7.04	8	4	87.0	9	42	1
1992	N.Y. Giants	4	137	83	60.6	912	6.66	5	3	83.3	6	17	0
1993	N.Y. Giants	16	400	247	61.8	3,038	7.60	15	9	88.3	28	31	0
Totals		**164**	**4,647**	**2,576**	**55.4**	**33,462**	**7.20**	**199**	**157**	**78.5**	**349**	**1,252**	**6**

Transactions
- Selected by New York Giants in first round (seventh pick overall) of the 1979 NFL Draft;
- On injured reserve with separated shoulder (Nov. 18–Dec. 26, 1981);
- On injured reserve with knee injury (Aug. 30–end of 1982 season);
- On injured reserve with foot injury (Dec. 18–end of 1990 season);
- On injured reserve with elbow injury (Oct. 14–end of 1992 season).

Noteworthy
- Selected to two Pro Bowls (following the 1985 and 1993 seasons);
- Starting quarterback in Giants' Super Bowl XXI victory;
- Completed 22 of 25 passes for 268 yards and 3 touchdowns and was named MVP in XXI;
- Was injured late in the regular season and did not play in Giants' Super Bowl XXV victory;
- His uniform number 11 was retired by the Giants;
- Holds records for highest completion percentage for a Super Bowl and postseason game (88.0);
- Tied for second in Super Bowl history for consecutive completions (10);
- Giants career leader in completions, passing yards, and touchdown passes;
- Most 300-yard passing games in Giants history (21);
- Set Giants record with 40 completions for 513 yards (at Cincinnati, Oct. 13, 1985);
- Came off the bench in the fifth game of his rookie season, earned the starting role, and led the Giants to victory in six of his first eight career starts;
- Son, Chris, is a quarterback and was selected in the 2003 NFL Draft;
- Announces NFL games, serving as an analyst on CBS' broadcast team.

KEN STABLER (for more information, see pages 64–65)

YEAR	TEAM	G	ATT	COMP	PCT	YDS	YPA	TD	INT	RATING	RUSHING		
											ATT	YDS	TD
1968	Oakland					DID NOT PLAY							
1969	Oakland					DID NOT PLAY							
1970	Oakland	3	7	2	28.6	52	7.43	0	1	18.5	1	-4	0
1971	Oakland	14	48	24	50.0	268	5.58	1	4	39.2	4	29	2
1972	Oakland	14	74	44	59.5	524	7.08	4	3	82.3	6	27	0
1973	Oakland	14	260	163	62.7*	1,997	7.68	14	10	88.3	21	101	0
1974	Oakland	14	310	178	57.4	2,469	7.96	26*	12	94.9	12	-2	1
1975	Oakland	14	293	171	58.4	2,296	7.84	16	24	67.4	6	-5	0
1976	Oakland	12	291	194	66.7*	2,737	9.41*	27*	17	103.4*	7	-2	1
1977	Oakland	13	294	169	57.5	2,176	7.40	20	20	75.2	3	-3	0
1978	Oakland	16	406	237	58.4	2,944	7.25	16	30	63.3	4	0	0
1979	Oakland	16	498	304	61.0	3,615	7.26	26	22	82.2	16	-4	0
1980	Houston	16	457	293	64.1	3,202	7.01	13	28	68.7	15	-22	0
1981	Houston	13	285	165	57.9	1,988	6.98	14	18	69.5	10	-3	0
1982	New Orleans	8	189	117	61.9	1,343	7.11	6	10	71.8	3	-4	0
1983	New Orleans	14	311	176	56.6	1,988	6.98	9	18	61.4	9	-14	0
1984	New Orleans	3	70	33	47.1	339	4.84	2	5	41.3	1	-1	0
Totals		**184**	**3,793**	**2,270**	**59.8**	**27,938**	**7.37**	**194**	**222**	**75.3**	**118**	**93**	**4**

*Led league

Transactions
- Selected by Oakland Raiders in the second round (52nd overall pick) of the 1968 AFL-NFL Draft
- Traded by Raiders to Houston Oilers for QB Dan Pastorini (March 17, 1980);
- Released by Oilers (July 15, 1982), signed by New Orleans Saints (Aug. 24, 1982).

Noteworthy
- Selected to four Pro Bowls (following the 1973, 1974, 1976, and 1977 seasons);
- 1974 NFL player of the year;
- Starting quarterback in Raiders' Super Bowl XI victory;
- Completed 12 of 19 passes for 180 yards and 1 touchdown in Super Bowl XI;
- Led Raiders to five consecutive AFC Championship Games (1973–77);
- Raiders career leader in passing yards (19,078) and touchdown passes (150);
- Participated in three famous plays: lofted 8-yard touchdown pass to Clarence Davis with 26 seconds left to give Oakland 28–26 victory over Miami in 1974 AFC Divisional Playoff Game; Davis' catch over outstretched Dolphins arms is called the "Sea of Hands"; in the 1977 AFC Divisional Playoff Game, the Raiders won thanks to his 42-yard pass to Dave Casper, also known as the "Ghost to the Post"; and in a 1978 game at San Diego, trailing 20–14 with time running out, Stabler purposely fumbled the ball forward…the Raiders kicked the ball toward the end zone until they recovered it for a game-winning touchdown, which is remembered as the "Holy Roller."

BART STARR (for more information, see pages 20–21)

YEAR	TEAM	G	ATT	COMP	PCT	YDS	YPA	TD	INT	RATING	RUSHING ATT	RUSHING YDS	RUSHING TD
1956	Green Bay	9	44	24	54.5	325	7.39	2	3	65.1	5	35	0
1957	Green Bay	12	215	117	54.4	1,489	6.93	8	10	69.3	31	98	3
1958	Green Bay	12	157	78	49.7	875	5.57	3	12	41.2	25	113	1
1959	Green Bay	12	134	70	52.2	972	7.25	6	7	69.0	16	83	0
1960	Green Bay	12	172	98	57.0	1,358	7.90	4	8	70.8	7	12	0
1961	Green Bay	14	295	172	58.3	2,418	8.20	16	16	80.3	12	56	1
1962	Green Bay	14	285	178	62.5*	2,438	8.55	12	9	90.7	21	72	1
1963	Green Bay	13	244	132	54.1	1,855	7.60	15	10	82.3	13	116	0
1964	Green Bay	14	272	163	59.9	2,144	7.88	15	4	97.1	24	165	3
1965	Green Bay	14	251	140	55.8	2,055	8.19	16	9	89.0	18	169	1
1966	Green Bay	14	251	156	62.2*	2,257	8.99*	14	3	105.0	21	104	2
1967	Green Bay	14	210	115	54.8	1,823	8.68*	9	17	64.4	21	90	0
1968	Green Bay	12	171	109	63.7*	1,617	9.46*	15	8	104.3	11	62	1
1969	Green Bay	12	148	92	62.2*	1,161	7.84	9	6	89.9	7	60	0
1970	Green Bay	14	255	140	54.9	1,645	6.45	8	13	63.9	12	62	1
1971	Green Bay	4	45	24	53.3	286	6.36	0	3	45.2	3	11	1
Totals		**196**	**3,149**	**1,808**	**57.4**	**24,718**	**7.85**	**152**	**138**	**80.5**	**247**	**1,308**	**15**

*Led league

Transactions
- Selected by Green Bay Packers in the seventeenth round (200th overall pick) of the 1956 NFL Draft.

Noteworthy
- Inducted into Pro Football Hall of Fame in 1977;
- 1966 NFL player of the year;
- Selected to four Pro Bowls (following the 1960–62 and 1966 seasons);
- Starting quarterback for five NFL titles and in Packers' Super Bowl I and II victories;
- Passed for 3 touchdowns in 1961 NFL Championship Game victory;
- Passed for 4 touchdowns in 1966 NFL Championship Game victory;
- Passed for 2 touchdowns and scored on winning 1-yard quarterback sneak with 13 seconds left to win 1967 NFL Championship Game, also known as "The Ice Bowl";
- Completed 16 of 23 passes for 250 yards and 2 touchdowns and was named MVP in Super Bowl I;
- Completed 13 of 24 passes for 202 yards and 1 touchdown and was named MVP in Super Bowl II;
- Also guided Packers to 1962 and 1965 NFL titles and a berth in 1960 championship game;
- His uniform number 15 was retired by the Packers;
- Owns highest career postseason passer rating (104.8);
- First in lowest percentage of postseason passes intercepted (1.41);
- Second for most consecutive passes without an interception (294 in 1964 and 1965);
- Later served as Packers' head coach (1975–1983).

ROGER STAUBACH (for more information, see pages 40–41)

YEAR	TEAM	G	ATT	COMP	PCT	YDS	YPA	TD	INT	RATING	RUSHING ATT	YDS	TD
1969	Dallas	6	47	23	48.9	421	8.96	1	2	69.5	15	60	1
1970	Dallas	8	82	44	53.7	542	6.61	2	8	42.9	27	221	0
1971	Dallas	13	211	126	59.7	1,882	8.92*	15	4	104.8	41	343	2
1972	Dallas	4	20	9	45.0	98	4.90	0	2	20.4	6	45	0
1973	Dallas	14	286	179	62.6	2,428	8.49*	23*	15	94.6*	46	250	3
1974	Dallas	14	360	190	52.8	2,552	7.09	11	15	68.4	47	320	3
1975	Dallas	13	348	198	56.9	2,666	7.66	17	16	78.5	55	316	4
1976	Dallas	14	369	208	56.4	2,715	7.36	14	11	79.9	43	184	3
1977	Dallas	14	361	210	58.2	2,620	7.26	18	9	87.0	51	171	3
1978	Dallas	15	413	231	55.9	3,190	7.72	25	16	84.9*	42	182	1
1979	Dallas	16	461	267	57.9	3,586	7.78	27	11	92.3*	37	172	0
Totals		**131**	**2,958**	**1,685**	**57.0**	**22,700**	**7.67**	**153**	**109**	**83.4**	**410**	**2,264**	**20**

*Led league

Transactions
- Selected by Dallas Cowboys in the 10th round (129th overall pick) of the 1964 NFL Draft;
- In military service (1965–68).

Noteworthy
- Inducted into Pro Football Hall of Fame in 1985;
- Selected to six Pro Bowls (following the 1973 and 1975–1979 seasons);
- Starting quarterback for four NFC titles and in Cowboys' Super Bowl VI and XII victories;
- Completed 12 of 19 passes for 119 yards and 2 touchdowns and was named MVP in VI;
- Completed 15 of 24 passes for 204 yards and 2 touchdowns in X;
- Completed 17 of 25 passes for 183 yards and 1 touchdown in XII;
- Completed 17 of 30 passes for 228 yards and 3 touchdowns in XIII;
- Did not play in Cowboys' Super Bowl V loss, but became starter midway through the following season and guided Dallas to four Super Bowls and six NFC East titles in nine seasons as a starter;
- Best passer rating in NFL history at the time of his retirement;
- A great clutch performer, Staubach led the Cowboys to 23 fourth-quarter comebacks, including 14 in the last two minutes of the game or in overtime;
- Nicknamed "Captain Comeback" for his last-minute heroics, and also tagged with the moniker "Roger the Dodger" for his elusiveness and ability to "dodge" opponents while in the pocket;
- Staubach won the 1963 Heisman Trophy as a junior at Navy, was drafted by the Cowboys in the spring of 1964, and played for Navy in the fall of 1964. How did this happen? Until 1966, the NFL allowed teams to draft a player whose "class" had graduated, even if the player had been redshirted, or transferred schools, and thus still had a fifth year of eligibility. Dallas drafted Staubach in 1964, watched him play his final season with the Midshipmen, then spend four years in the Navy (including a stint in Vietnam) before joining the franchise in 1969.

FRAN TARKENTON (for more information, see pages 42–43)

YEAR	TEAM	G	ATT	COMP	PCT	YDS	YPA	TD	INT	RATING	RUSHING ATT	RUSHING YDS	RUSHING TD
1961	Minnesota	14	280	157	56.1	1,997	7.13	18	17	74.7	56	308	5
1962	Minnesota	14	329	163	49.5	2,595	7.89	22	25	66.9	41	361	2
1963	Minnesota	14	297	170	57.2	2,311	7.78	15	15	78.0	28	162	1
1964	Minnesota	14	306	171	55.9	2,506	8.19	22	11	91.8	50	330	2
1965	Minnesota	14	329	171	52.0	2,609	7.93	19	11	83.8	56	356	1
1966	Minnesota	14	358	192	53.6	2,561	7.15	17	16	73.8	62	376	4
1967	N.Y. Giants	14	377	204	54.1	3,088	8.19	29	19	85.9	44	306	2
1968	N.Y. Giants	14	337	182	54.0	2,555	7.58	21	12	84.6	57	301	3
1969	N.Y. Giants	14	409	220	53.8	2,918	7.13	23	8	87.2	37	172	0
1970	N.Y. Giants	14	389	219	56.3	2,777	7.14	19	12	82.2	43	236	2
1971	N.Y. Giants	13	386	226	58.5	2,567	6.65	11	21	65.4	30	111	3
1972	Minnesota	14	378	215	56.9	2,651	7.01	18	13	80.2	27	180	0
1973	Minnesota	14	274	169	61.7	2,113	7.71	15	7	93.2	41	202	1
1974	Minnesota	13	351	199	56.7	2,598	7.40	17	12	82.1	21	120	2
1975	Minnesota	14	425*	273*	64.2	2,994	7.04	25*	13	91.8	16	108	2
1976	Minnesota	13	412	255*	61.9	2,961	7.19	17	8	89.3	27	45	1
1977	Minnesota	9	258	155	60.1*	1,734	6.72	9	14	69.2	15	6	0
1978	Minnesota	16	572*	345*	60.3	3,468*	6.06	25	32	68.9	24	-6	1
Totals		**246**	**6,467**	**3,686**	**57.0**	**47,003**	**7.27**	**342**	**266**	**80.4**	**675**	**3,674**	**32**

*Led league

Transactions

- Selected by Minnesota Vikings in the third round (29th overall pick) of the 1961 NFL Draft;
- Traded by Vikings to N.Y. Giants for a first- (Clinton Jones) and second-round pick (WR Bob Grim) in the 1967 NFL Draft, a first-round pick (T Ron Yary) in the 1968 draft, and a second-round pick (G Ed White) in the 1969 draft (March 8, 1967);
- Traded by N.Y. Giants to Vikings for QB Norm Snead, WR Bob Grim, RB Vince Clements, a first-round choice (DE Larry Jacobson) in the 1972 NFL Draft and a second-round pick (LB Brad Van Pelt) in the 1973 draft (1972).

Noteworthy

- Inducted into Pro Football Hall of Fame in 1986;
- Selected to nine Pro Bowls (following the 1964, 1965, 1967–1970, and 1974–76 seasons);
- 1975 NFL player of the year;
- Starting quarterback for three NFC championships and six consecutive NFC Central titles;
- His uniform number 10 was retired by the Vikings;
- At the time of his retirement, Tarkenton held NFL records for: career and single-season completions (345 in 1978); career touchdown passes (342); and career passing yards (47,003);
- Tarkenton, Ron Yary, and Ed White, who were each involved in the 1967 trade of Tarkenton, were all selected to the Vikings' 40th Anniversary Team.

Y.A. TITTLE (for more information, see pages 82–83)

											RUSHING		
YEAR	TEAM	G	ATT	COMP	PCT	YDS	YPA	TD	INT	RATING	ATT	YDS	TD
1948	Balt. (AAFC)	14	289	161	55.7	2,522	8.73	16	9	90.3	52	157	
1949	Balt. (AAFC)	11	289	148	51.2	2,209	7.64	14	18	66.8	29	89	
1950	Baltimore	12	315	161*	51.1	1,884	5.98	8	19	52.9	20	77	
1951	San Francisco	12	114	63	55.3	808	7.09	8	9	68.2	13	18	
1952	San Francisco	12	208	106	51.0	1,407	6.76	11	12	66.3	11	-11	
1953	San Francisco	11	259	149	57.5	2,121	8.19	20	16	84.1	14	41	
1954	San Francisco	12	295	170	57.6	2,205	7.47	9	9	78.7	28	68	
1955	San Francisco	12	287	147	51.2	2,185	7.61	17*	28	56.6	23	114	
1956	San Francisco	10	218	124	56.9	1,641	7.53	7	12	68.6	24	67	
1957	San Francisco	12	279	176*	63.1*	2,157	7.73	13	15	80.0	40	220	
1958	San Francisco	11	208	120	57.7	1,467	7.05	9	15	63.9	22	35	
1959	San Francisco	11	199	102	51.3	1,331	6.69	10	15	58.0	11	24	
1960	San Francisco	9	127	69	54.3	694	5.46	4	3	70.8	10	61	
1961	N.Y. Giants	13	285	163	57.2	2,272	7.97	17	12	85.3	25	85	
1962	N.Y. Giants	14	375	200	53.3	3,224	8.60	33*	20	89.5	17	108	
1963	N.Y. Giants	13	367	221	60.2*	3,145	8.57*	36*	14	104.8	18	99	
1964	N.Y. Giants	14	281	147	52.3	1,798	6.40	10	22	51.6	15	-7	
NFL Totals		**178**	**3,817**	**2,118**	**55.5**	**28,339**	**7.42**	**212**	**221**	**73.6**	**291**	**999**	**3**
AAFC Totals		**25**	**578**	**309**	**53.5**	**4,731**	**8.19**	**30**	**27**	**78.6**	**81**	**246**	
Totals		**203**	**4,395**	**2.427**	**55.2**	**33,070**	**7.52**	**242**	**248**	**74.3**	**372**	**1,245**	**3**

*Led league

Transactions

- Signed by Cleveland Browns of the AAFC (December 1947);
- Selected by Detroit Lions in the first round (sixth overall pick) of the 1948 NFL Draft, but did n sign with the Lions;
- Rights transferred to Baltimore Colts (1948);
- Colts franchise merged into NFL (1950);
- Colts franchise disbanded, players made available in 1951 draft, and Tittle selected by 49ers in first round (third overall pick) of the 1951 NFL Draft;
- Traded by 49ers to N.Y. Giants for G-LB Ed Cordileone (1961).

Noteworthy

- Inducted into Pro Football Hall of Fame in 1971;
- 1963 NFL player of the year;
- Selected to seven Pro Bowls (following the 1953, 1954, 1957, 1959, and 1961–63 seasons);
- Led the Giants to three consecutive NFL championship games (1961–63);
- His uniform number 14 was retired by the Giants, despite playing just four seasons for them;
- The Colts were the worst team in the AAFC in 1947, so other clubs gave the Colts some players for the 1948 season; one of the players given to the Colts was Tittle.

JOHNNY UNITAS (for more information, see pages 84–85)

YEAR	TEAM	G	ATT	COMP	PCT	YDS	YPA	TD	INT	RATING	RUSHING ATT	YDS	TD
1956	Baltimore	12	198	110	55.6	1,498	7.57	9	10	74.0	28	155	1
1957	Baltimore	12	301*	172	57.1	2,550*	8.47	24*	17	88.0	42	171	1
1958	Baltimore	10	263	136	51.7	2,007	7.63	19*	7	90.0	33	139	3
1959	Baltimore	12	367*	193*	52.6	2,899*	7.90	32*	14	92.0	29	145	2
1960	Baltimore	12	378*	190*	50.3	3,099*	8.20	25*	24	73.7	36	195	0
1961	Baltimore	14	420*	229	54.5	2,990	7.12	16	24	66.1	54	190	2
1962	Baltimore	14	389	222	57.1	2,967	7.63	23	23	76.5	50	137	0
1963	Baltimore	14	410	237*	57.8	3,481*	8.49	20	12	89.7	47	224	0
1964	Baltimore	14	305	158	51.8	2,824	9.26*	19	6	96.4	37	162	2
1965	Baltimore	11	282	164	58.2	2,530	8.97*	23	12	97.4	17	68	1
1966	Baltimore	14	348	195	56.0	2,748	7.90	22	24	74.0	20	44	1
1967	Baltimore	14	436	255	58.5*	3,428	7.86	20	16	83.6	22	89	0
1968	Baltimore	5	32	11	34.4	139	4.34	2	4	30.1	3	-1	0
1969	Baltimore	13	327	178	54.4	2,342	7.16	12	20	64.0	11	23	0
1970	Baltimore	14	321	166	51.7	2,213	6.89	14	18	65.1	9	16	0
1971	Baltimore	13	176	92	52.3	942	5.35	3	9	52.3	9	5	0
1972	Baltimore	8	157	88	56.1	1,111	7.08	4	6	70.8	3	15	0
1973	San Diego	5	76	34	44.7	471	6.20	3	7	40.0	0	0	0
Totals		**211**	**5,186**	**2,830**	**54.6**	**40,239**	**7.76**	**290**	**253**	**78.2**	**450**	**1,777**	**13**

*Led league

Transactions
- Selected by Pittsburgh Steelers in the ninth round (102nd overall pick) of the 1955 NFL Draft;
- Released by Steelers (Sept. 1955), signed as free agent by Baltimore Colts (1956);
- Traded by Colts to San Diego Chargers for $150,000 (Jan. 22, 1973).

Noteworthy
- Inducted into Pro Football Hall of Fame in 1979;
- 1964 and 1967 NFL player of the year;
- Owns distinction of having been selected to more Pro Bowls (10, following the 1957–1964 and 1966–67 seasons) than any other quarterback;
- Starting quarterback for Colts' 1958 and 1959 NFL titles as well as Super Bowl V triumph;
- Guided the Colts to victory in "The Greatest Game Ever Played," the 1958 NFL Championship Game, in which he passed for a then-postseason-record 361 yards;
- Completed then-Super Bowl record 75-yard touchdown pass to John Mackey in Super Bowl V;
- His uniform number 19 was retired by the Colts;
- Set NFL record for most consecutive games with a touchdown pass (47, the next closest player has thrown a touchdown pass in 30 consecutive games);
- Retired as all-time leader in passing yards and touchdown passes;
- After being released by Steelers in 1955, Unitas played semipro football for the Bloomfield Rams in the Pittsburgh area while working construction before signing with Colts in 1956.

NORM VAN BROCKLIN (for more information, see pages 86–87)

YEAR	TEAM	G	ATT	COMP	PCT	YDS	YPA	TD	INT	RATING	RUSHING ATT	RUSHING YDS	RUSHING TD
1949	Los Angeles	8	58	32	55.2	601	10.36	6	2	111.4	4	-1	0
1950	Los Angeles	12	233	127	54.5	2,061	8.85*	18	14	85.1	15	22	1
1951	Los Angeles	12	194	100	51.5	1,725	8.89	13	11	80.8	7	2	2
1952	Los Angeles	12	205	113	55.1*	1,736	8.47*	14	17	71.5	7	-10	0
1953	Los Angeles	12	286	156	54.5	2,393	8.37	19	14	84.1	8	11	0
1954	Los Angeles	12	260	139	53.5	2,637*	10.14*	13	21	71.9	6	-10	0
1955	Los Angeles	12	272	144	52.9	1,890	6.95	8	15	62.0	11	24	0
1956	Los Angeles	12	124	68	54.8	966	7.79	7	12	59.5	4	1	1
1957	Los Angeles	12	265	132	49.8	2,105	7.94	20	21	68.8	10	-4	4
1958	Philadelphia	12	374*	198*	52.9	2,409	6.44	15	20	64.1	8	5	1
1959	Philadelphia	12	340	191	56.2	2,617	7.70	16	14	79.5	11	13	2
1960	Philadelphia	12	284	153	53.9	2,471	8.70	24	17	86.5	11	-13	0
Totals		**140**	**2,895**	**1,553**	**53.6**	**23,611**	**8.16**	**173**	**178**	**75.1**	**102**	**40**	**11**

*Led league

Transactions
- Selected by Los Angeles Rams in the fourth round (37th overall pick) of the 1949 NFL Draft;
- Traded by Rams to Philadelphia Eagles for G-T Buck Lansford, CB Jimmy Harris, and a first-round pick (RB Dick Bass) in the 1959 NFL Draft (1958).

Noteworthy
- Inducted into Pro Football Hall of Fame in 1971;
- Co-1960 NFL player of the year;
- One of two players to retire after winning player of the year award (Jim Brown was the other);
- Selected to nine Pro Bowls (following the 1950–55 and 1958–1960 seasons);
- Starting quarterback on two NFL title teams (1951 and 1960);
- With the 1951 NFL Championship Game tied in the fourth quarter, Van Brocklin fired a 73-yard touchdown pass to Tom Fears to give the Rams the winning 24–17 margin;
- Passed for 1 touchdown as the Eagles handed Green Bay coach Vince Lombardi his only postseason loss in the 1960 NFL Championship Game;
- Still holds NFL single-game record for passing yards (554, vs. N.Y. Yanks, Sept. 28, 1951);
- Shares Rams record for most games with at least 4 touchdown passes (6);
- Tied for third in NFL history for most seasons leading league in average gain per pass (3);
- Served as his team's punter for final 10 seasons, posting a career 42.9 average;
- Led the NFL in punting in 1954 and 1955;
- Shared quarterback duties his first four seasons with fellow future Pro Football Hall of Fame member Bob Waterfield;
- Retired after 1960 season and became head coach of the expansion Minnesota Vikings;
- Was Vikings coach for six seasons, and also served as head coach of the Falcons (1968–1974).

MICHAEL VICK (for more information, see pages 44–45)

YEAR	TEAM	G	ATT	COMP	PCT	YDS	YPA	TD	INT	RATING	RUSHING ATT	YDS	TD
2001	Atlanta	8	113	50	44.2	785	6.95	2	3	62.7	31	289	1
2002	Atlanta	15	421	231	54.9	2,936	6.97	16	8	81.6	113	777	8
Totals		**23**	**534**	**281**	**52.6**	**3,721**	**6.97**	**18**	**11**	**77.6**	**144**	**1,066**	**9**

*Led league

Transactions
- Selected by Atlanta Falcons in the first round (first overall pick) of the 2001 NFL Draft.

Noteworthy
- Selected to one Pro Bowl (following the 2002 season);
- Became just sixth quarterback since 1970 to be voted to the Pro Bowl in his first season as starter;
- Set NFL single-game record by a quarterback for rushing yards (173 at Minnesota, Dec. 1, 2002);
- Set NFL single-game record by averaging 17.3 yards per carry (10 carries for 173 yards at Minnesota, Dec. 1, 2002);
- Owns the second- and fourth-best two-game rushing totals by a quarterback, since 1970, in NFL annals (193 yards, Nov. 24-Dec. 1, 2002 and 182 yards, Oct. 20–27, 2002);
- First quarterback in NFL history to post consecutive games with at least 90 rushing yards (91 yards vs. Carolina, Oct. 20, 2002, and 91 yards at New Orleans, Oct. 27, 2002);
- His 46-yard touchdown run in overtime (at Minnesota, Dec. 1, 2002) was the longest run ever by a Falcons quarterback;
- Set Falcons single-season record for rushing touchdowns by a quarterback (8 in 2002);
- Guided Falcons to 27–7 victory in a 2002 NFC Wild Card Game at Green Bay. Falcons became first team to defeat Packers in a playoff home game (had been 13–0 at home);
- Third in NFL history for rushing yards by a quarterback in a season (777 in 2002);
- Most rushing yards by a quarterback after two seasons (1,066);
- Scored on 3 touchdown runs of at least 30 yards in 2002;
- Third in Falcons history in most consecutive passes without an interception (171);
- Was a backup to Chris Chandler in 2001, played in eight games, and started twice;
- A day before the 2001 NFL Draft, the Falcons traded three draft picks and WR Tim Dwight to the San Diego Chargers for the rights to select Vick;
- First African-American quarterback selected with first overall draft choice;
- After redshirting his freshman year, played just two seasons at Virginia Tech;
- Guided Virginia Tech to 11–0 regular-season record as a freshman in 2000, led the nation in passer efficiency, and finished third in Heisman Trophy voting (matching the highest finish for a freshman). Was injured part of his sophomore season, but finished with a 20–1 record as a starter;
- Dolphins Pro Bowl cornerback Sam Madison: "[Vick's] best athlete in the NFL. It doesn't always matter how well you defend a receiver. His arm is so good that he can throw the ball right past you."

KURT WARNER (for more information, see pages 114–115)

YEAR	TEAM	G	ATT	COMP	PCT	YDS	YPA	TD	INT	RATING	RUSHING ATT	RUSHING YDS	RUSHING TD
1998	St. Louis	1	11	4	36.4	39	3.55	0	0	47.2	0	0	0
1999	St. Louis	16	499	325	65.1*	4,353	8.72*	41*	13	109.2*	23	92	1
2000	St. Louis	11	347	235	67.7*	3,429	9.88*	21	18	98.3	18	17	0
2001	St. Louis	16	546	375*	68.7*	4,830*	8.85*	36*	22	101.4*	28	60	0
2002	St. Louis	7	220	144	65.5	1,431	6.50	3	11	67.4	8	33	0
Totals		**51**	**1,623**	**1,083**	**66.7**	**14,082**	**8.68**	**101**	**64**	**98.2**	**77**	**202**	**1**

*Led league

Transactions
- Signed as a undrafted free agent by the Green Bay Packers (April 28, 1994);
- Released by Packers (August 1994), played for Arena League's Iowa Barnstormers (1995–97);
- Signed by St. Louis Rams (Dec. 26, 1997).

Noteworthy
- 1999 and 2001 NFL player of the year;
- Selected to three Pro Bowls (following the 1999–2001 seasons);
- Starting quarterback for two Super Bowls, including Rams' victory in XXXIV;
- Completed 24 of 45 passes for 414 yards and 2 touchdowns and was named MVP in Super Bowl XXXIV;
- Completed 28 of 44 passes for 365 yards and 1 touchdown in Super Bowl XXXVI;
- His 414 passing yards in Super Bowl XXXIV are a single-game Super Bowl record;
- Completed a game-winning 73-yard touchdown pass to Isaac Bruce with 1:54 left in Super Bowl XXXIV to snap a 16–16 tie and give Rams first NFL title in 48 years (since 1951);
- Leading passer in NFL history (98.2 career passer rating);
- Tied NFL record for consecutive 300-yard passing games (6);
- Second in NFL single-season history in passing yards (4,830 in 2001);
- Third in NFL single-season history in touchdown passes (41 in 1999);
- Fifth in NFL single-season history in passer rating (109.2 in 1999);
- Completed 28 of 44 passes for 365 yards and 1 touchdown in XXXVI;
- Missed five games in 1999 with broken finger, and missed nine games in 2002 with broken hand;
- Earned opportunity to start when Trent Green was injured in a 1999 preseason game;
- Signed with the Rams in December 1997, and was sent to play for the NFL Europe League's Amsterdam Admirals in 1998. Warner led in the NFLEL in passing yards and touchdowns;
- Played three seasons (1995–97) with Iowa Barnstormers of the Arena League, where he passed for 10,486 yards and 183 touchdowns;
- Stocked shelves at an Iowa grocery store to supplement income while with Barnstormers;
- Signed with Green Bay Packers out of college, and was in 1994 training camp with Brett Favre, Mark Brunell, and Ty Detmer before being released.

BOB WATERFIELD (for more information, see pages 88–89)

YEAR	TEAM	G	ATT	COMP	PCT	YDS	YPA	TD	INT	RATING	RUSHING ATT	YDS	TD
1945	Cleveland Rams	10	171	89	52.0	1,609	9.41*	14*	17	72.4	18	18	5
1946	Los Angeles	11	251*	127*	50.6	1,747	6.96	17*	17	67.6	16	-60	1
1947	Los Angeles	12	221	96	43.4	1,210	5.48	8	18	39.2	3	6	1
1948	Los Angeles	11	180	87	48.3	1,354	7.52	14	18	60.0	7	12	0
1949	Los Angeles	12	296	154	52.0	2,168	7.32	17	24	61.3	5	-4	1
1950	Los Angeles	12	213	122	57.3*	1,540	7.23	11	13	71.7	8	14	1
1951	Los Angeles	11	176	88	50.0	1,566	8.90*	13	10	81.8	9	49	3
1952	Los Angeles	12	109	51	46.8	655	6.01	3	11	35.7	9	-14	1
Totals		**91**	**1,617**	**814**	**50.3**	**11,849**	**7.33**	**97**	**128**	**61.6**	**75**	**21**	**13**

Led league

Transactions

- Selected by Cleveland Rams in the fifth round (42nd overall pick) of the 1944 NFL Draft;
- Rams franchise moved to Los Angeles (1946).

Noteworthy

- Inducted into Pro Football Hall of Fame in 1965;
- 1945 NFL player of the year;
- Selected to two Pro Bowls (following the 1950–51 seasons. The Pro Bowl was not played for the 1945–49 seasons);
- Rams won two NFL titles and four division titles during his tenure;
- Only rookie starting quarterback to win NFL championship (1945);
- Passed for 2 touchdowns in 1945 NFL Championship Game victory;
- His uniform number 7 was retired by the Rams;
- A great all-around athlete, Waterfield served as the Rams punter and kicker. He twice led the NFL in field-goal percentage, twice led the league in extra-point percentage, and averaged 42.4 yards per punt for his career;
- He also grabbed 20 interceptions in four seasons as a two-way (offensive and defensive) player;
- The Rams had not posted a winning season prior to Waterfield's arrival, when they had a 9–1 record and won the 1945 NFL title;
- Second in NFL history for average gain per pass attempt by rookie (9.41 in 1945);
- Shared quarterback duties with Norm Van Brocklin from 1949–1952;
- Just as Roger Staubach was a future choice by the Cowboys (see page 158), Waterfield was selected by the Rams in 1944 but went back to UCLA that fall and then joined the Rams in 1945;
- Was married to movie star Jane Russell.

DOUG WILLIAMS (for more information, see pages 22–23)

YEAR	TEAM	G	ATT	COMP	PCT	YDS	YPA	TD	INT	RATING	RUSHING ATT	YDS	TD
1978	Tampa Bay	10	194	73	37.6	1,170	6.03	7	8	53.4	27	23	1
1979	Tampa Bay	16	397	166	41.8	2,448	6.17	18	24	52.5	35	119	2
1980	Tampa Bay	16	521	254	48.8	3,396	6.52	20	16	69.9	58	370	4
1981	Tampa Bay	16	471	238	50.5	3,563	7.56	19	14	76.8	48	209	4
1982	Tampa Bay	9	307	164	53.4	2,071	6.75	9	11	69.6	35	158	2
1983						SIGNED WITH USFL							
1984	Oklahoma (USFL)	15	528	261	49.4	3,084	5.84	15	21	60.5	28	89	3
1985	Arizona (USFL)	17	509	271	53.2	3,673	7.22	21	17	76.4	27	82	1
1986	Washington	1	1	0	0.0	0	0.00	0	0	39.6	0	0	0
1987	Washington	5	143	81	56.6	1,156	8.08	11	5	94.0	7	9	1
1988	Washington	11	380	213	56.1	2,609	6.87	15	12	77.4	9	0	1
1989	Washington	4	93	51	54.8	585	6.29	1	3	64.1	1	-4	0
NFL Totals		**88**	**2,507**	**1,240**	**49.5**	**16,998**	**6.78**	**100**	**93**	**69.4**	**220**	**884**	**15**
USFL Totals		**32**	**1,037**	**532**	**51.3**	**6,757**	**6.52**	**36**	**38**	**68.3**	**55**	**171**	**4**
Totals		**120**	**3,544**	**1,772**	**50.0**	**23,755**	**6.70**	**136**	**131**	**69.1**	**275**	**1,055**	**19**

*Led league

Transactions
- Selected by Tampa Bay Buccaneers in the first round (17th overall pick) of the 1978 NFL Draft;
- Granted free agency, signed with USFL's Oklahoma's Outlaws (Aug. 8, 1983);
- USFL rights traded by Boston Breakers to Oklahoma Outlaws for rights to RB Cliff Chatman an a future draft pick (Oct. 11, 1983);
- On injured reserve with knee injury (June 4–end of 1984 season);
- Protected in merger of Oklahoma Outlaws and Arizona Wranglers (Dec. 6, 1984);
- Granted free agency when USFL suspended operations (Aug. 7, 1986), re-signed by Buccaneers and traded to Washington Redskins for fifth-round pick (CB Tony Mayes) in the 1987 NFL Draf (Aug. 13, 1986);
- On nonfootball injury list with appendectomy (Sept. 22–Oct. 21, 1988);
- On reserve/nonfootball injury list with back injury (Aug. 29–Nov. 3, 1989).

Noteworthy
- First African-American quarterback drafted in the first round;
- First African-American quarterback to start a Super Bowl game;
- Completed 18 of 29 passes for 340 yards and 4 touchdowns and was named MVP in XXII;
- Set still-standing Super Bowl marks by passing for 228 yards and 4 touchdowns in one quarter (second quarter) en route to the Redskins' 42–10 victory in XXII;
- The Buccaneers had won just 2 games in their first two seasons prior to Williams' arrival in 1978 With Williams at quarterback, the Buccaneers reached the postseason three times in five seasons. Williams left after the 1982 season, and the franchise did not return to the playoffs until 1997.

STEVE YOUNG (for more information, see pages 46–47)

YEAR	TEAM	G	ATT	COMP	PCT	YDS	YPA	TD	INT	RATING	RUSHING ATT	RUSHING YDS	RUSHING TD
1984	L.A. (USFL)	12	310	179	57.7	2,361	7.62	10	9	80.6	79	515	7
1985	L.A. (USFL)	13	250	137	54.8	1,741	6.96	6	13	63.1	56	368	2
1985	Tampa Bay	5	138	72	52.2	935	6.78	3	8	56.9	40	233	1
1986	Tampa Bay	14	363	195	53.7	2,282	6.29	8	13	65.5	74	425	5
1987	San Francisco	8	69	37	53.6	570	8.26	10	0	120.8	26	190	1
1988	San Francisco	11	101	54	53.5	680	6.73	3	3	72.2	27	184	1
1989	San Francisco	10	92	64	69.6	1,001	10.88	8	3	120.8	38	126	2
1990	San Francisco	6	62	38	61.3	427	6.89	2	0	92.6	15	159	0
1991	San Francisco	11	279	180	64.5	2,517	9.02*	17	8	101.8*	66	415	4
1992	San Francisco	16	402	268	66.7*	3,465	8.62*	25*	7	107.0*	76	537	4
1993	San Francisco	16	462	314	68.0	4,023	8.71*	29*	16	101.5*	69	407	2
1994	San Francisco	16	461	324	70.3*	3,969	8.61*	35*	10	112.8*	58	293	7
1995	San Francisco	11	447	299	66.9*	3,200	7.16	20	11	92.3	50	250	3
1996	San Francisco	12	316	214	67.7*	2,410	7.63	14	6	97.2*	52	310	4
1997	San Francisco	15	356	241	67.7*	3,029	8.51*	19	6	104.7*	50	199	3
1998	San Francisco	15	517	322	62.3	4,170	8.07	36*	12	101.1	70	454	6
1999	San Francisco	3	84	45	53.6	446	5.31	3	4	60.9	11	57	0
NFL Totals		**169**	**4,149**	**2,667**	**64.3**	**33,124**	**7.98**	**232**	**107**	**96.8**	**722**	**4,239**	**43**
USFL Totals		**25**	**560**	**316**	**56.4**	**4,102**	**7.33**	**16**	**22**	**72.8**	**135**	**883**	**9**
Totals		**194**	**4,709**	**2,983**	**63.3**	**37,226**	**7.91**	**248**	**129**	**94.0**	**857**	**5,122**	**52**

*Led league

Transactions
- Selected by Los Angeles Express in the first round (tenth overall pick) of the 1984 USFL Draft;
- Selected by Tampa Bay Buccaneers in the first round (first pick overall) of the 1984 NFL Supplemental Draft;
- Released by Express (Sept. 9, 1985), signed by Buccaneers (Sept. 10, 1985);
- Traded by Buccaneers to San Francisco 49ers for second-round (LB Winston Moss) and fourth-round (WR Bruce Hill) picks in the 1987 NFL Draft and cash (April 24, 1987).

Noteworthy
- Selected to seven Pro Bowls (following the 1992–98 seasons);
- Named 1992 and 1994 NFL player of the year;
- Starting quarterback for 49ers' Super Bowl XXIX victory;
- Completed 24 of 36 passes for 325 yards and record 6 touchdowns, rushed for a game-high 49 yards, and was named MVP in Super Bowl XXIX;
- Owns single-season passer rating record (112.8 in 1994);
- Posted a passer rating greater than 100 a record six times. Next closest is Joe Montana with three 100-point passer rating seasons;
- Tied for most seasons leading league in passer rating (6);
- Ranks second all-time in career passer rating and rushing yards by a quarterback.

PHOTO CREDITS

SOURCES

Statistical information was provided by various sources, including *Total Football II* and the *2003 NFL Record & Fact Book*.

ABOUT THE AUTHOR

Matt Marini is an Associate Editor for NFL Creative, based in Los Angeles. He is the editor of the *NFL Record & Fact Book*.